Wisdom With Understanding is Better Than Rubies

Lurine Karon Greenberg Fine Arts Collection

NEW TENT ARCHITECTURE

NEW TENT ARCHITECTURE

NEW TENT ARCHITECTURE PHILIP DREW

Thames & Hudson

[p. 2] Chemical Research Centre, Venafro (Italy). Samyn & Partners, architects.

First published in 2008 in hardcover in the United States of America by Thames & Hudson Inc., 500 Fifth Avenue, New York, New York 10110

thamesandhudsonusa.com

Library of Congress Catalog Card Number 2007904765

ISBN 978-0-500-34243-5

Design by SMITH
Lesley Gilmour, Victoria Forrest
smith-design.com

Printed and bound in Singapore by C S Graphics Pte Ltd

ARCHITECTURE ON THE MOVE
Philip Drew

There are two distinct types of architecture: the first is permanent, fixed and costly, all straight lines and square openings cut into solid planes or rectangular skeletons of concrete, steel and glass; and the second is so lightweight and ephemeral, so utterly different in its curved shapes without a straight line visible anywhere, that it hardly warrants the term 'architecture'. But it is this second type of building – textile architecture in tension – that is the subject of this book.

Not everyone likes tents. On the front page of a newspaper, the headline reads: 'A tents relationship with the kids'. The article underneath points out that older Australians would rather live in a tent than move in with their grown-up children, a revealing comment on how little liked tents were when it comes to housing. We pity anyone forced to live in a tent: circus performers, gypsies, refugees, soldiers, victims of earthquakes and cyclones. Only the desperate or the very poor inhabit tents, and none willingly. Tents represent a last resort, when all else has failed. This negative opinion of tents is pervasive, and the discovery that tents were previously recognized as a symbol of heaven is a shock to most people. The cosmos was in fact once visualized as a great tent within a tent. In the past, tents were far from miserable affairs, with some even serving as magnificent mobile palaces for powerful rulers and kings.

Tents, therefore, encompass both the lowest and the highest in architecture. Today, new trends in tensile architecture are quietly resolving this ancient paradox by making tents stronger, more durable and beautiful, whilst preserving such traditional traits as their lightness, flexibility and structural efficiency without sacrificing spatial transparency and freedom. Tents, above all else, make great sculptures. They are soft, sensuous, feminine, touchable, adaptable, compact, easily dismantled and relocated, and convenient. The distrust of tents in the West still affects our response to fabric buildings today, whether a traditional tent or an advanced membrane structure that employs the very latest materials and technologies. Tents possess a remarkable and unique heritage as the solution to the human need for mobility brought on by climatic stress, and consequently they ought to inform and guide our understanding of how the new tent architecture can reduce our consumption of materials and energy.

Readers who become familiar with the typical shapes and features of tents will quickly recognize their imitation in monumental architecture. Gothic cathedrals, with their flying buttresses that reflect the angled profile of restraining guy ropes, are in essence fossilized tents, in which tent shapes are reproduced in more permanent materials. They are much more prevalent than one might suppose. The crossover between the milieu of traditional tents and monumental building is symptomatic of the cross-fertilization of civilized culture by nomads, and demonstrates how fluid the relationship is between hard and soft architecture as it oscillates back and forth between two extremes. Consequently, it is sometimes difficult to determine whether a structure is a tent or a representation of a tent in stone, concrete or steel. 'Civilization', it was once remarked by no less an authority than Kenneth Clark, consists of books and stone buildings, and tents, therefore, which belonged to the realm of the barbarian nomads and warrior clans, had no legitimate place in cities. But, as will become apparent, this is changing.

With its lightweight textile cover, the tent was an obvious metaphor for an invisible city and sanctuary for the human soul. Recent tent architecture often appropriates this symbolism without consciously recognizing what is meant, since we have lost touch with the tent's earlier nomadic association following its assimilation into settled societies. But tent symbolism is too potent to ever be forgotten entirely. With our mobile lifestyles, tents, far from representing an outmoded genre, are increasingly relevant as practical solutions to urgent building needs.

New Tent Architecture is about much more than tent symbolism, which is relevant only insofar as it affects how we unconsciously approach modern membrane building. This is a story about recent innovations in shapes and materials, and in the way in which tents

[opposite] **Large architectural umbrellas are now widely used in outdoor spaces. Federal Garden Show, Cologne (Germany), 1971. Frei Otto, architect.**

are designed. The pace of innovation was uneven, development was confined to Germany and America, and spread from there to regions such as Japan, the Middle East, and later Asia. Why Germany, and why, to a lesser degree, America? What was it about their cultures that favoured modern tent architecture? And why are the most spectacular examples found in countries such as Saudi Arabia, Kuwait and Qatar, while a country like France, which was so deeply infected by the crusades and its tent symbolism, has lagged behind? Other factors besides the more obvious technical and engineering ones were clearly at work.

The 20th-century emphasis on engineering and chemistry in Germany is only part of the explanation. Post-war shortages did spur structural innovation, most notably in the design of stayed bridges, but the combination of Romanticism in the 19th century followed by Expressionism in the early part of the 20th century cannot be dismissed as symptomatic of a deeper quest for new forms linked to nature. Neoclassicism, and indeed monumentality generally, was tainted by its connection with Hitler and the Nazis. In the wake of war and defeat, Germany required a new style. The anti-monumental imagery of Frei Otto's tents supplied an aesthetic purgative, taken up with considerable enthusiasm, which also corresponded to the early modern glass

architecture movement. The West Germany Pavilion at Expo 67 in Montreal and, more widely, the transparent Plexiglas cable-net roofs of the Munich Olympic Games in 1972 offered a new architectural expression that was the exact antithesis of totalitarian monumentality. Backing anti-monumental visual transparency was Germany's historically important chemical industry – including companies such as Hoechst – for whom membrane architecture was a great opportunity to become the supplier of the necessary synthetic yarns.

In the US, the suspension bridge was an important technological achievement and symbol of the progressive, adventurous spirit of the country in the second half of the 19th century and the early 20th century. But even American tensile structure possessed a German connection: John Augustus Roebling (1806–69), the architect behind the Brooklyn Bridge, was born at Mülhausen and received his engineering education at the Royal Polytechnic Institute in Berlin, where Frei Otto would later study. It is no coincidence that important membrane fabricators such as Vector-Foiltec, Toray Deutschland, Covertex and Skyspan are located in Germany. The production of fibreglass fabrics is highly centralized; Chemfab in the US is the only important non-German fabricator.

English involvement came later with the collaboration of Ted Happold of engineering firm Arup with Frei Otto in the 1970s. This late entrée into tensile architecture is puzzling given the Tudors' 16th-century leadership in luxurious royal tents, and the assimilation of tents into English social and sporting life, from cricket to horse races. It is possible that membrane architecture looked too risky; Happold, after all, was a maverick. It was Millennium Project funding that eventually gave the new tent the push it needed. In the Commonwealth nation of Australia, strong sunlight and an architectural history inflected by verandas as shaded extensions to the house encouraged the adoption of fabric shade roofs. These could be regarded as a continuation of the traditional veranda, which, by shading outside rooms, provided a transitional link with the landscape.

Their appearance is radical yet familiar – radical because the shapes are unfamiliar, but familiar because they obey well-established tensile structural behaviours. Across Western Europe and North America, and more recently the Middle East, Japan and the new Asian tigers, Korea and China, super-tents proliferate as authentic landmarks of progress. Large mega-tents are expensive prestige constructions that signal a message of industrial and technical progress and economic success to the outside world.

In the late 1970s and early 1980s, a new era in membrane structures was ushered in by stronger, coated woven fabrics that were more durable and had increased performance. In the fast-moving economies of the West, a service life of twenty to thirty-five years was economically acceptable. This new membrane architecture now competed with conventional heavy construction: it used less material, went up faster, had a lighter and cheaper support structure, and the membranes could be prefabricated away from the building site. Not only was their performance superior, they were also cost competitive. A decade after the 1972 Munich Olympics, a huge (425,250m²), Teflon-coated, fibreglass fabric super-roof for the Haj Terminal in Jeddah by Skidmore, Owings & Merrill marked a milestone in the size and quality of membrane canopies. In the US, sales of fabric for all structural uses grew by 40 per cent between 1978 and 1979. In the long-span market alone, sales increased seven-fold – a considerable proportion due solely, no doubt, to the Haj Terminal. But the use of cheap membranes, together with poor fabrication and welded joints, could result in failure. Where in the past such failures could be repaired on

But it was the Japanese who were most naturally at ease with membranes. They were not afraid of impermanence, and beauty was all the more admired because it was fleeting. This ready acceptance of the ephemeral encouraged firms such as Taiyo Kogyo to commit heavily for Expo 70 at Osaka, and in fact many of the Expo fabric structures were designed by leading Japanese architects. Taiyo Kogyo's roof for Davis, Brody, Chermayeff's low cable-restrained US Pavilion, one of the first clear-span, air-supported roofs ever built, in particular was much admired.

Woven fabric or foil material tents are currently designed with the latest computer software to analyze load and stress conditions. The previously limited range of shapes has expanded greatly, and these new tents look radically different from their traditional predecessors. Such advances have occasioned a great leap forward in the functionality and scale of the new tent architecture. As a revolution it has been a relatively quiet affair, accompanied by a complete transformation of the design, materials, engineering, performance and applications of membrane structures. Whereas before they were small constructions, tents have grown in size, durability and engineering complexity to the point where they compete with and surpass conventional buildings. The new super-tents are actually mega-tents – a new architectural species – which cover huge spaces.

[above] US Pavilion, Expo 70, Osaka (Japan). Davis, Brody, Chermayeff, architects.

[right] Haj Terminal, King Abdul Aziz International Airport, Jeddah (Saudi Arabia), 1980. Skidmore, Owings & Merrill, architects.

the spot by hand, now the entire membrane had to be replaced. The new sophisticated, high-performance materials were fabricated to exacting standards under stringently controlled conditions, and a mistake in the sizing and cutting of a panel or cable could disrupt construction and lead to long and costly delays. At the Sony Centre (p. 162) in Berlin, for example, escaping hydraulic fluid from a broken tower crane hose spilled onto the PTFE Sheerfill V fabric valley elements and ruined them, potentially delaying completion.

This book explores the new frontiers of tent architecture and illustrates the many ways in which designers have responded to integrating structural form with the emerging lightweight aesthetic. It also provides essential information on membrane structures, how they are designed and fabricated, and showcases outstanding recent examples around the world, explaining how they were designed so that architects will be able to collaborate more effectively with engineers on their own lightweight projects. My aim is to inform architects, students, and anyone with an interest in fabric applications about this exciting structural medium, and to encourage a greater appreciation for it. Only when the basic principles, advantages, behaviours and limits of fabric structures are fully understood will their potential be confidently realized.

Traditional nomadism may be a thing of the past, but it is being replaced by a new urban nomadism as young people embrace mobility and the new microelectronic technologies. Freed from the constraints of the workstation, these 21st-century nomads circulate through the city, meeting people, doing work, celebrating life, while staying in touch with family, friends and colleagues. All this is being realized with the advent of mobile phones, digital cameras, iPods and MP3 players, with the result that we are all beginning to look like electro-gadget pack mules. No other architectural type satisfies this desire to be liberated and mobile as completely as the tent, which can be modified, taken down, packed, transported and re-erected using less energy and wasting fewer resources than other forms of architecture. The bulk and weight of conventional buildings is an obstacle in a society

driven by economic and cultural change at an ever-increasing pace: office towers designed to last forty years must now be refurbished at ten- to fifteen-year intervals to remain competitive.

The world today is challenged by a combination of factors, including climate change, exploding population numbers and rising resource and energy costs, all of which make unprecedented demands on architects to design more effective and sustainable buildings. Tents, which were originally a response to resource deprivation, contain many lessons for today's looming ecological crisis. In 1969, pop architecture group Archigram anticipated an era of ultimate personal mobility with their Monaco Entertainments Centre competition entry. Their scheme included buildings that would walk and floors that would slide up and down, and looked forward to plug-in electronic communications nodes in the landscape. Everything, like the nomad, would be mobile. But even this radical vision seems rather conservative when compared with today's reality. Our world has moved even faster: walking buildings aren't necessary when the city itself is on the move.

Nothing symbolizes the world of the urban nomad better than the new tent architecture. Ours is a paradoxical age full of contradictions as our physical world dissolves into a digital miasma, and our consumption of material goods rises. While architecture is often claustrophobic and imprisoning, tents were never like that. The new membrane structures are lighter, more open, less constrained and more liberating than anything that has come before. Buildings do walk, and as people venture more and more into the outdoors they become less and less reliant on architecture. In an era of globalization, the new tent symbolizes a Zeitgeist whose essence is a lighter, mobile, connected world of information and communication. At their most ethereal, tents invade streets and squares and fill the city with the ghosts of nomads past. You might even say that the tent has come in from the desert into the heart of our cities.

TENTS AS ARCHITECTURE

The King caused a tent of vermilion silk, very elegant and richly made, to be pitched in the fields on the same spot where he had been granted the truce, then dismissed all his men.
Jean Froissart, *Chronicles*, 1377

Are tents architecture?

A little less than 600 years after Jean Froissart wrote his *Chronicles*, the question 'what is architecture?' would have assumed great urgency for the architectural historian Nikolaus Pevsner, with London crashing down around him during the Blitz. His answer in 1941 that 'a bicycle shed is a building; Lincoln cathedral is a piece of architecture' would undoubtedly have resonated at a time when the very fabric of civilization was being pulverized into charred rubble. 'The term architecture', he declared, 'applies only to buildings designed with a view to aesthetic appeal.' Since then, its meaning has been expanded by the likes of Bernard Rudofsky, Reyner Banham and Robert Venturi, but 'architecture' continues to signify primarily permanent buildings made out of stone, concrete and glass. But omitting tents from architectural history leads to one that is exclusively a narrative about monumental buildings.

To be thought of as architecture, tents must be more than useful or structurally efficient – they must also, according to Pevsner,

[above, right] **Damascus from the Barada River (Syria). 19th-century engraving.**

[right] **Majnun before Layli's tent, from** *Jami's Seven Thrones*, *c.* **1556–1665. Freer Gallery of Art, Washington, DC (USA).**

[opposite] **David takes the cup and spear while Saul sleeps in his tent, from the Morgan Bible, folio 34 (recto),** *c.* **1250. The Pierpont Morgan Library, New York, New York (USA).**

be beautiful. The beauty of tents is all the more striking because it is integral to and expressive of nomadism. Monumental buildings will continue to be important key symbols of civilization; modern membrane constructions merely enlarge what we mean by it. Tents are the by-products of a wandering tribal existence that has largely disappeared. As such, they are closer to life than architecture, and are as beautiful and saturated with symbols as much as any building can be. Where they are different is in their durability and in the amount of material used to make them.

What else is different about tents? Conceptually, tents enclose space, convey important aesthetic and cultural messages, and are part of religious symbol systems. Well before interior space was made permanent with the monumental temple architecture of Ancient Egypt, it is present in tents. What sets tents apart is their portable character: the lightness, translucency and portability of fabric all dovetail with the requirement for mobility. Unlike the austere castles of stone along the Rhine or the Loire, the famed luxury tents of the Outremer (12th- and 13th-century feudal states in Asia Minor and the Holy Land) were magnificent and comfortable accommodations that seduced many a crusader knight.

Nomads and history

The relationship of nomads to city civilizations is complex: they possess a profound cosmological outlook, implicitly accepted, which impressed itself upon their immediate springs of action. Their fate is frequently intertwined with cities, often as antagonists, but all too often nomads are vilified as the enemies of civilization. Most of us know about the Arab incursion in Europe and defeat at Poitiers in 732 and the later invasion by the Golden Horde in 1241, but we tend to be less interested in the role of nomads as bridges between great civilizations, as traders and merchants carrying valuable goods and innovations. Nomads played a positive and indispensable role in linking distant civilizations. As conquerors, they have been responsible for some of the most sensitive and elegant

officers in a brilliant setting of tents; atop the city wall are the defiant Viennese citizenry. An empty field separates the two combatants. It is an image which supports the widespread European perception of nomads and tents as the dark face of civilization. But Süleyman's tents were gorgeous portable palaces, more splendid than many of the stone or wooden structures that crowded behind the Viennese wall. Ottoman Sultans deployed two identical tents that leapfrogged each other, ensuring that a newly pitched accommodation was ready at the end of the day's journey. Tents featured at important diplomatic receptions and played an integral role in urban ceremonial life long after the Osmanli Turks ceased to be nomads.

From the Ancient Egyptians to the Assyrians and on down to the Romans, and until quite recently, armies have relied on tents during military campaigns. These campaign tents were exquisite creations: Egyptian tent poles, for example, were often gilded and decorated with precious stones, and the tent of the Assyrian king, Sennacherib (705–681 BC), contained folding chairs and portable furniture. Tents were part of an aggressive military culture from the outset. This by its very nature was fundamentally different to the architecture of Ancient Egypt with its temple shrines and funereal monuments, which were treated as sculptural objects placed within a limitless space. Architecture in the beginning was essentially religious, and tents were functional shelters that coexisted alongside this monumental tradition.

The picture that emerges of nomads is one of interdependent, rather than separate, cultures, sharing a much greater range of contacts than has generally been acknowledged. Conquests included rich empires, which they ruled and transformed, and words like 'balcony', 'cupola', 'divan', 'frieze', 'ogive' and 'sofa' recall the Arab contribution to architecture. Another notable contribution was the integration of architecture, to which they brought a certain delicacy and lightness of touch, and garden design. The use of water in enclosed gardens is just one illustration of the idea that palace and garden should be one. The French 'pavilion'

architecture created by any people. It is important to recognize that the boundary between city and nomad is porous: the two economies serve each other and intertwine to the benefit of both.

It is an absurd distortion to dismiss nomads as uncivilized or to say they lacked architecture; masterpieces such as the Alhambra and La Mezquita, both in Spain, prove the contrary. Nor can it be truly said that nomads are entirely arrested societies: successive waves of Arabs and Berbers conquered Spain, the Hsiung-nu, Hsien-pei and Tolsa tribes overran China, the Ottomans mastered Turkey, and the Mughals (under Babar the Great) dominated northern India. All created rich architectural traditions and had a creative impact on the civilizations they conquered, bringing with them new ideas and introducing plants, irrigation and administrative systems, language, sports and foods. The tent was possibly the least of their gifts. The clash of nomadic and city cultures is depicted in a painting by an anonymous Turkish artist of the siege of Vienna, which occurred on 27 September 1529. Behind a line of cannon, Süleyman the Magnificent confers with his is in fact an imitation tent placed in a garden. The idea was to connect man's activities with nature, a reference to the nomad's open-air tent experience on the steppes, surrounded by the scent of flowers and the sight of birds and animals. Persian miniature manuscript paintings vividly recollect this dimension of the nomad's delight in nature.

Tents and cultural resistance zones

Tents originated in what are termed 'cultural resistance zones', marginal arid or desert regions with meagre resources. The inhabitants of such areas were often from more favourable regions, driven out or dispossessed by aggressive invaders. Cultural resistance zones are stressful regions, sometimes frigid but more often hot and dry. They are challenging and make extreme demands on human adaptability. Here, geography is destiny as people are forced to move in search of water and pasture. Tents, which required minimal material and energy for transport, represented a logical solution to resource-deficient environments and became a necessity. Over many centuries, they have been refined and perfected to the point where only what is essential to their erection, maintenance and transport remains.

Tents, therefore, are among the cheapest and most efficient structures on the planet. No other traditional shelter is as structurally effective or as lightweight. Some nomadic peoples, including Eskimos, possess as many as four tents for the different seasons. Tents are what one would expect of a people whose survival is predicated on moving about. Their lightweight construction reduces to a minimum the material needed for their construction, which would be sourced from the herd. Being made from woven fabric, they are light and easily folded, lessening the bulk and energy needed for transport. Circus big tops illustrate how this works, while time and motion studies conducted by the American military during the Second World War proved the tent's operational efficiency.

The importance of permanence?

Behind the clash of urban and nomadic cultures lies a much deeper divide: the dichotomy of permanence and impermanence. In everyday life we are frequently offered a choice between opposites: tent or temple, eternal or provisional? What is missing from this duality is the recognition that tents developed gradually from wattle-and-daub huts into skin-and-felt dwellings, and ultimately into a diverse series of stretched textile structures. Wanderers divested themselves of anything that was extraneous because each extra kilogram carried came with a cost. Relying instead on oral traditions, nomads still possessed music, art and literature, just simply less of it.

But even nomads looked to eternity and occasionally built stone monuments, such as the late 12th- and 13th-century tombs at Erzurum in Turkey, which repeated the shapes of Tartar tents. In Egypt, the Heb-Sed chapel monuments at Saqqara are copies of even earlier mat-covered tents. What is especially interesting is the representation of tents, which are transient, in monuments of stone to suggest permanence and continuity. Buildings preceded books as dynastic records and objects for religious imagery: in *The Hunchback of Notre Dame* (1831), Victor Hugo suggested that cathedrals served as stone books before the portable printed variety superseded them. In this sense, a printed book is the lightweight portable equivalent of a tent. We are now witnessing something analogous in the replacement of books by laptop computers. Even in advanced civilizations such as our own, the balance between stasis and mobility has shifted; laptops replace offices and convert people into urban nomads.

The contest between a desire for stable permanent symbols and a contrary desire for freedom strikes a different balance depending on the times. Too much change can cause a craving for stability; too much stability, and the pendulum swings in the opposite direction and people wish for greater change and adventure. And so it goes. The movement of nomads and their flocks is cyclical and follows seasonal

patterns. Eliminate the tent, and the nomad's way of life is destroyed. Not only are the nomad's tents superbly crafted to suit a nomadic life of constant movement, the materials used are obtained from the pastoral economy, and, in turn, express the minimal existence of the wandering herdsman's life, whether he is a Greenland Inuit or a Bedouin of the Great Sandy Desert.

In the present day, materials that were introduced in the 1950s now extend the service life of fabric structures; no longer are they strictly temporary. The new synthetic woven textiles and coatings offer stronger, longer-lasting, self-cleaning membranes. The increase in the permanence of membranes in the 1980s and 1990s ushered in an exciting period in which tents began to come into their own as semi-permanent structures. This made them far more acceptable and announced the beginning of a new era of maturity in tent architecture.

Structural efficiency

Kilogram for kilogram, tents are among the most structurally effective forms of shelter. The reason is simple: tent membranes distribute their loads by tension, using the same principle as a sailor's hammock. The imposed loads flow through the structure. In framed structures, load and resistance are hidden; we have little visual sense as to how loads are directed. It is possible to actually 'feel' the forces in the shapes of the membrane because it is so structurally articulate. In the late 16th century, European explorers were struck by the speed and manoeuvrability of the kayaks of the Greenland Inuit. Made of sealskin stretched over frameworks, they darted around in the water much faster than any European boat could travel. The 5.8m-long boats were individually tailored to the paddler's size, weight and arm length. Like clothing, it was 'worn' by its owner; sealskin with watertight seams is lashed around the hole in the craft where the paddler sits, preventing ice-cold water from splashing over the deck. The Inuit kayak is just a further example of how mobility tailored a more efficient lightweight membrane structure over much heavier European boat construction. If it works for boats, why not for architecture?

Traditional tents offered similar advantages of lightness, mobility and ease of transport. They, too, could be dismantled and loaded onto animals quickly in times of danger, and erected at another location when the danger had passed. In uncertain times, this meant survival. Tents are, in effect, large garments. Arab dress offers a clue: the long black or white cotton robes worn by Arab women, covering the body from head to toe, are indispensable shelters from the sun and leave room for air to circulate and the skin to perspire. Tents are merely larger versions of this loose second skin. Both tents and clothing insulate and shade, deflect wind and rain, protect modesty and convey social status. Both utilize similar weaving techniques, and textile tent cloths, like clothing, can be folded and stored readily. Tents can be thought of as a more generous version of a large kaftan, accommodating more than one body and allowing movement within.

In a storm, a tent's skin will stretch and relax and flap, helping to dissipate wind energy by reducing the radius of curvature and stress. This is one of the main differences of fabric as a building material to masonry or timber. The collapse of a monumental building happens without warning because it is unyielding. Unlike conventional rigid buildings that limit movement, such movement is normal in fabric structures and allows the cloth to shed imposed loads. Contemporary membranes behave in a similar manner. It may be disconcerting to be surrounded by walls that move and floors that sway, but this is perfectly natural in tensile buildings and is critical to their survival.

The exterior glass walls of Frei Otto's Institute for Lightweight Structures in Vaihingen, near Stuttgart, continually shifted and rocked in response to movements in the roof. The exposed cables underneath the timber inner cladding pulled tight or extended, depending on the wind- or snow-load, and the wall mullions reacted accordingly. The building, resembling a long-necked dinosaur from a distance, was a large, cable-net tent that flexed and moved according to the loads and forces acting on it. Not only did it look organic, inside it behaved more like

[above] **Institute for Lightweight Structures, Vaihingen (Germany), 1968. Frei Otto, architect.**

[opposite] **Federal Garden Show, Cologne (Germany), 1957, with the cathedral in the background. Frei Otto, architect.**

a living creature. If the wings of a commercial aircraft did not flex, they would be so heavy that the plane would not take off. We accept this, but not in buildings. Movement redistributes imposed loads in the tent membrane. We are so accustomed to buildings being relatively rigid that we are shocked when they move. But it is important to realize that it is the movement in a membrane that makes it safe. After all, sailors manage stress in a similar manner by pulling in or letting out the sails of boats.

With tents being woven clothing on a larger scale, it was a short step from making clothes to weaving tents and, consequently, it was natural that the tent should be identified with the womenfolk. With the men spending much of the day away from camp tending the herd, it was more practical for the tent to be made and cared for by the women. During Bedouin tribal battles, the women quickly dismantled the camp and retreated to a secret location to await the outcome. Turning the tent over to the women freed the men to defend the group.

Architecture is unassailably masculine, distant and hard. We approach it slowly. But tents are quite different. They are soft, resilient, responsive, qualities they have in common with clothing. This link of tents to clothing, though it has lessened today, distinguishes contemporary membrane architecture from monumental building. Like an overcoat, tents are flexible containers of people. This underlying feminine quality contrasts with the heavy male stance of monumental architecture. It is one reason people find membrane structures more approachable yet strangely difficult to accept. Acceptance of the new tent into the mainstream will require a shift in consciousness, which is not inconceivable given the growing influence of women in contemporary society. One is tempted to say it is long overdue. Yet in the hands of male architects and engineers, the feminine character of the new membrane structures has been noticeably de-emphasized to make them appear more masculine. This present danger should be addressed before the new tent architecture drifts away from its true tent nature and becomes more rigidly male.

A tent aesthetic

Tents possess a distinct and innate aesthetic, summed up by their feminine character and minimalist lightness. The horizontal dimension dominates, a look we easily recognize in such structures as the suspension bridge and the Bedouin tent. Because the shapes are curved, non-aggressive and enveloping, we see them as feminine, although the suspension bridge, with its huge bestriding span, has an air of conquest that is more assertively masculine. In considering a black tent, with its wonderful carpet floor and hanging screens that divide the interior space, it is impossible not to sense that it makes a strong and quite different aesthetic statement to monumental architecture. The most perfect synthesis of this aesthetic is encountered in Persian miniature images of tent life, which convey the tent's form, rich decoration and spatial openness centuries ahead of Frank Lloyd Wright's prairie houses or Mies van der Rohe's experiments in the late 1920s. Tents embodied the boundless freedom of the steppe, but it took modern architecture to appreciate the spatial freedom of the tent, with its insubstantial floating canopies that strongly connect the interior with the outside landscape. The tent was new and revolutionary, yet ancient.

Unlike monumental architecture, the tent form is about tension rather than weight. The woven tent cloth is patterned with stripes and geometric designs, an abstractness which is appealingly modern. Lightweight construction makes the tent more efficient. And because the material weighs so little, tents have an unearthly quality as though gravity has been cancelled. The weight of the membrane is so small as to be negligible, and so lightweight that sunlight penetrates through it, precluding the presence of windows. Consequently, we are much more aware of the outside. Nature is closer at hand and, at the same time, the reduction in material means that the barrier to the outside is less. We live with nature in tents and not separate from it, as is the case in thick-walled buildings with their collections of imprisoning cells, not unlike beehives. The aesthetic has its origin in the close connection between nomad and nature.

Tents help us to retain the landscape, and to live with it on more intimate terms. Apart from its quite different spatial culture, tents also offer a different set of references to landscape than are found in urban architecture – more open, more adaptable, less intrusive. The reduction in material and lightness informs how tents sit in nature. There is no platform, no stylobate such as one encounters in Greek temples. They stand directly on the ground, with no heavy, obstructive walls to isolate the inside, and are essentially stretched figures, so that the predominant dimension is horizontal. In Assyrian bas-reliefs, the horizontality of tents was deliberately compressed to save stone, but in reality they whirled across the landscape as lightly as dancers. Even when brightly coloured with strong patterns, tents don't really stand out as their flowing curves echo the outlines of the landscape. Their long profiles and horizontal spreading stance blend into the countryside and its rhythms; the fabric may sweep upwards and echo a distant mountain range, or it may repeat the line of a sand dune behind it. The diversity in the shapes of black tents associated with North Africa, the Middle East and Tibet allow them to be identified with the particular regions and landscapes in which they are found.

Nomads accustomed to living outside in close contact with nature preferred light, flexible spaces, such as those found in the open porches of Ali Qapu, overlooking the Maidan at Isfahan, in Iran. Nomad architecture, whether it is the Alhambra in Spain or Fatehpur Sikri in India, is unusually sensitive in the way that it is connected by light and sudden vistas to nature. Indeed, the planning of the palace at Fatehpur Sikri is said to have derived from Arab and Central Asian tent encampments. The modern pavilion, with its sliding or retractable glass walls, seeks a comparable opening up to the outside.

The allure of tents

Not only do tents represent something exotic and different, they also possess an indefinable allure. The roofs of Viennese palace buildings imitate Ottoman tents, and as far as afield as Drottingholm, outside Stockholm, there are splendidly painted copper replicas of Ottoman guard tents. The tent of the Middle East suggested a luxurious hidden world, a quality that is at the heart of the tent's exoticism in music, opera and art. Demonizing Arab and Ottoman cultures only heightened this exoticism in the European imagination. What did the muslin veil hide? In an excessively masculine Europe, the culture of the tent exposed a lost feminine component, a more open sexuality that was less rigidly controlled, which both tantalized and threatened adventurers like Sir Richard Burton and T.E. Lawrence, among many others. Because they originated elsewhere, tents have become an almost archetypal signifier of the outsider. Fabric structures supply a dramatic foil to city monumentality, their curvilinear shapes the perfect retort to the monotony of rectangles. In the end, it amounts to the simple opposition of the ephemeral versus the eternal via the opposition of fabric and stone.

The tent way of life is so different that its allure can be reduced to something as pervasive and fundamental as the biological opposition between male and female, encapsulated in the contrast between fabric's innate sensuality, suppleness and softness, responsiveness to touch, and subtle echo of its surroundings. The feminine tent is a ready-made partner of masculine architecture. In a European culture trapped in extreme masculine projection, the representation of femininity by the tent is especially seductive. Tents are more alive in their reaction to wind, sun, storms, night, morning, evening: they breathe. The exclusion of tents from the mainstream was a mistake. They are too important, useful and valuable to be dismissed in this way. It goes well beyond structural efficiency and economy to a wholly different set of underlying values and symbolism. We can learn so much from the tent's relationship to ourselves and to nature, and the mysterious connection it exercises between matter and spirit. To see this at its most sublime, we need only visit the dome of the Sala de las dos Hermanas at the Alhambra. By a clever trick, the dome splinters into a myriad of frozen scintillations, crystal-like fragments that pierce

[opposite, above] Shade-net protection over a large residential area.

[opposite, below] Shade nets for agriculture. 'Shade in the desert', 1972. Atelier Warmbronn, architects, with Büro Rolf Gutbrod and Arup.

the veil separating the physical universe from a metaphysical one of unfathomable immensity. Reality is an illusion, all things pass. Western architecture grappled with this idea in the ribbed vaults of Gothic cathedrals, frescoed Baroque ceilings and the minimalism of Modernism. Tents took the nomad there thousands of years before in the desert.

Modernist imitations

Nothing demonstrates the enduring fascination tents exercise more than their imitation in the 20th century. Their extreme structural economy made them a model of human constructional ingenuity. In Modernist architecture the tent took different forms, both literally (as a tensile structure) and figuratively (as imitation monumental architecture that was sculptural and symbolic). Eero Saarinen employed tent motifs for several projects, including the huge, curving concrete sheet at Dulles International Airport (1958–62), near Washington, DC, but used modern structural means. Following Saarinen, Kenzo Tange created some of the most memorable large-scale tents of the 20th century for the 1964 Tokyo Olympic Games. Because the shapes were not purely tensile, these structures are rightly viewed as tent sculptures. Tange's swimming stadium fused traditional Japanese temple roof forms with Saarinen's roof for the hockey rink at Yale University using shipbuilding technology, whereas Jørn Utzon's concrete hanging roofs for the superb Kuwait National Assembly building (1972–82) were rigid versions of Saarinen's roof at Dulles, alluding to the Bedouin black tents in which his client's forebears had lived prior to establishing themselves at the edge of the Persian Gulf.

Massimiliano Fuksas's glass-and-steel roof draped over the 1,300m-long walkway for the 2005 Milan Trade Fair also mimicked tent shapes. This huge, undulating, transparent glass canopy bisected the complex, with its eight exhibition halls to each side, and created a luminous glow that was visible everywhere. Underneath the glass, the space felt abnormally ethereal; above, the glass surface alternately swept upwards into cone-shaped peaks, or was pulled downwards as funnel downdrafts. The big difference between Fuksas's surface and Frei Otto's membrane pavilion for Expo 67 nearly forty years earlier is that the latter was an actual stretched cable-net with fabric underneath it, while the former consisted of supported glass panels.

Challenges and opportunities

The evidence for climate change now appears incontrovertible. Hurricane Katrina in September 2005, the hottest month for 125 years, was an unwelcome reminder, as are the ongoing problems of retreating glaciers, prolonged droughts, bleached coral reefs and disappearing species. For thousands of years, tents were the chosen form of shelter because they made sparing use of resources, while providing shade in hot arid regions. Now, these traditional tents suggest more efficient ways of building. We need to think about our world with the same careful regard as the nomads did. Reducing greenhouse gas emissions will mean a diminution of fossil fuels, cutting down energy use and single-cycle materials. Buildings are already being designed that are more sustainable, but much more needs to be done. In *Walden*, Henry David Thoreau observed: 'Consider first how slight a shelter is absolutely necessary . . . I have seen Penobscot Indians in this town, living in tents of thin cotton cloth, while the snow was nearly a foot deep around them, and I thought that they would be glad to have it deeper to keep out the wind.' The enlarged hole in the ozone layer over the Antarctic exposes more and more of us to harmful solar radiation, and outdoor membrane shade canopies and nets can provide additional protection in these circumstances.

Building efficiently is just as critical in the present day as it was for Eskimos in the Arctic tundra or for Bedouin tribesmen struggling to survive on the arid margins of the desert. Tents are pure environmental structures. All buildings modify the environment, but because they must work in extreme conditions, tents are more exclusively protective. Japanese architecture and the minimalism of Modernism demonstrate that paring architecture down to its bare essentials

enhances, rather than decreases, its power to express. Less is truly more. Apart from the tent's structural truthfulness, its skin is translucent to sunlight during the day. At night, every interior object is projected on the walls and roof in silhouette. One of the memorable spectacles of Expo 67 was Frei Otto's West Germany Pavilion at night. Its appearance changed completely after sunset: when the inside lights were switched on, the cable-net and fabric skin was converted into a giant Chinese lantern. Like recumbent Cinderellas, tents are transformed into glamorous princesses in glass slippers after dark. Monumental buildings tend to die visually just when tents are at their liveliest, alive with light and movement.

Not only is the new tent minimal, it is a special architecture with an Arab pedigree. Its position at the opposite end of the architectural spectrum only adds to its interest. To have become as important as it has, the new tent had to overcome a host of prejudices. Rich in new possibilities, it is becoming more and more relevant to a world struggling to cope with changes that threaten the very limits of the planet. In a world of six billion people (expected to grow to over 9.4 billion by 2050), against a backdrop of accelerating climate change, the example of nomad optimization of scarce resources is a lesson we ignore at our peril.

Symbolism

In Paul Theroux's novel *The London Embassy* (1982), the narrator describes a strange discovery:

> Fighting my way through a tangle of bushes I saw the tent. It was a sort of oriental tent, perhaps Arab, with slanting roof and high steep sides flowing down from neatly scalloped eaves. I thought for a moment I had stumbled upon a group of campers . . . But the tent was made of stone, with carved folds, and it bore a tablet with the name Captain Sir Richard F. Burton. The explorer's tomb was the strangest I had ever seen . . . This tomb, this stone tent, had a window.

Built to convey ideas rather than for practical purposes, monumental tents of stone such as the one described by Theroux are the products of an ancient symbolism that underlies the use of tents in the present day. Memorials like Burton's (located in Mortlake, Surrey) appropriate two important concepts: the tent as a metaphor for

[above, left] Monument to Absalom, Kidron Valley, near Jerusalem (Israel), 1st century BC.

[above, right] West Germany Pavilion, Expo 67, Montreal (Canada). Frei Otto, architect.

[opposite, left] Assyrian cavalry attack and set fire to Bedouin tents, 7th century BC.

[opposite, right] A crimson tent belonging to Henry VIII. From MS 3: Cotton Augustus, folio 18, 16th century. British Library, London (UK).

nomadic life, and the tent as an image of heaven as a separate place in the afterlife. Burton's tomb is not unique. Similar tombs, such as the monument to Absalom in the Kidron Valley outside Jerusalem, with its beautifully rendered parasol-roof tent, are found scattered throughout the Middle East. A symbol is an association between two different things that, on the surface, seem to be unconnected. The choice of a symbol enlarges our perception of the character of its subject. Nomads identified the tent with the dome of heaven, a veil between this life and the afterlife, and in medieval Christian iconography an encampment of tents symbolized heaven and the New Jerusalem. It also signified the soul's journey through this life.

The earliest tent images occur in battlefield scenes, from representations of Rameses II's camp as it is overrun by Hittite cavalry (1285 BC) to Assyrian bas-reliefs that graphically describe the massacre of Bedouin tribesmen as Ashurbanipal's cavalry set their collapsing black tents on fire (644 BC). Tents entered Europe in the 13th century in the aftermath of the crusades (1095–1204), and ever since pavilions have been associated with kingship. It was in France particularly that the discovery of a luxury tent culture led to this romantic connection of tents with knightly chivalry and tournaments. Eastern pavilions often appeared in European images of the crusades, including the siege of Constantinople and the capture of Jerusalem, among other battle scenes. The chivalric revival in the 16th century led to the production of magnificent tents of a scale that eclipsed anything seen previously. Such lavishness was

ostentatiously on view at the meeting of Francis I and Henry VIII at the Field of the Cloth of Gold in 1520. One of the most splendid works of English architecture was a magnificent 46m-long crimson tent, decorated in a gesture of diplomacy with both French fleur-de-lis and Tudor roses, from the early 16th century. Its spine of four pavilions was linked by low galleries, flanked on either side by five sets of parasol-roofed tents. Along the central ridge, a series of eighteen carved royal beasts surmount the tent poles.

France was an influential source of much tent symbolism. The poet and troubadour Chrétien de Troyes (d. *c.* 1183) introduced a green-and-vermilion pavilion in a beautiful meadow to symbolize the rape of Jerusalem, and there are frequent references to rich tents in Jean Froissart's 14th-century *Chronicles*. Tent details proliferated in castle turrets and in the elaborated roofscapes of the châteaux of the French nobility. The churches, too, of medieval France had tents buried within their masonry, and pavilion imagery was applied to reliquaries, canopies and roofs. At salient points, details of the essential inner tent push through the stone skin – a tent pole thrusts out from a buttress, topped by a climactic gold ball *pinot*. The decorative patterns of cloth were also sometimes imprinted in the stone. The Old Testament Tabernacle was an important idea in the Christian conception of cathedrals as a model of a dematerialized church fabric, from stained-glass 'curtains' to the lightness of the sanctuary, which adopted a similar pavilion geometry. Symbolically, the medieval cathedral is a stone tent. With its stained-glass walls

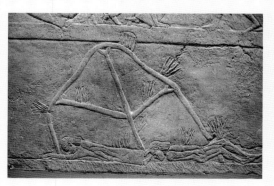

inside and inclined flying buttresses outside, the Gothic cathedral is a veritable tent that takes us back to the original Tabernacle.

This imitation of tents in stone may seem odd, but it was a fashionable idea that survived long after the crusades in the form of tented beds and interiors. In sacred architecture, earlier styles and details could often be seen that were unrelated to the building material, a notion that goes back thousands of years to Ancient Egypt, where column capitals repeated the forms of bundles of papyrus, and Greece, were masonry temples imitated earlier timber models. The tent may have been outside the European experience, but its imitation is little different to the imitative historicism of the ancient world. Later buildings continued the tradition of churches as stone tents. Balthasar Neumann's Church of the Holy Cross at Etwashausen, near Kitzingen-am-Main, with its sky-blue tiled pavilion straddling the crossing, harks back to medieval tent symbolism and reflects the three draped roofs surmounting the nave of St Barbara at Kutná Hora, Czechoslovakia, begun at the end of the 14th century, while the swooping, tent-like form of Giovanni Michelucci's concrete S. Giovanni Battista (1962) beside the Autostrada del Sole outside Florence is a reminder that the passing motorists are the modern mechanized counterparts of nomads. Tent symbolism rests on the contradiction that tents are ephemeral but signify an eternal heaven. The tent's lightness and translucency mirrored the journeying souls of men. What before this had been a portable shelter for nomads became the eternal abode

of God in heaven. This is a remarkable elevation for such a humble shelter.

Contemporary symbolism

This medieval tent symbolism is now nine centuries old. It should be extinct by now, or at least senescent, but the tent is a natural metaphor for a distinct and separate spiritual universe. Tent symbolism has survived the decline of religion in a materialist age and been reinvented to suit modern tastes, emerging in the poetry of William Blake, Robert Frost and T.S. Eliot, among others. It can surface unexpectedly, notably in David Storey's 1969 play *The Contractor*, which begins with actors pitching a wedding marquee on stage in front of the audience, and ends with the marquee being struck, packed up and loaded onto a truck. The raising and lowering of the tent signifies the life of the old tent-maker Ewbank, but is also used to describe a world holding an entire society with the loaded grace notes of the English class system. The tent here indicates a very English world. The wedding marquee itself, in which the marriage sacrament is celebrated within a tabernacle, is a survival from an earlier age when royal progresses required lavish tentage and monarchs were accompanied by troupes of courtiers and retainers. The king and his entourage were housed in splendid pavilions, for which the sergeant-of-tents was responsible. The tradition reached its zenith with the meeting of Francis I and Henry VIII at Ardes in 1520, and continues with the more modest events of today, such as polo matches and horse shows.

The symbolic meaning of the Egyptian hieroglyph for 'tent' denoted something which envelops, a symbolism closely connected with weaving and clothes. In the Middle Ages, tents signified a great many things that have been lost today. The structure and material of the tent has advanced, but its symbolism has retreated. New building types exist, and stronger, longer-lasting fabrics have been introduced. The really surprising thing in all this is the universality of the tent. From Skidmore, Owings & Merrill's giant Haj Terminal at Jeddah to Frei Otto's sports hall for King Abdul Aziz University (1981), to

Fentress Bradburn's Denver International Airport (p. 92), the old tent, greatly enlarged and made from new materials, has kept its connection to its Arab antecedents and wide desert spaces. This is true for much of the new tent architecture. Robert Frost's poem *The Silken Tent* (1942) is a wonderful summary of the tent's various meanings, emphasizing its feminine qualities, its sacredness and its silent aliveness. The tent membrane separates worlds and envelops like a garment. Whether we see it as a highly symbolic sacred stone tent or a modern super-tent, recent applications variously perpetuate aspects of the ancient and sacred, and, one is tempted to say, seminal meaning of the tent.

> She is as in a field a silken tent
> At midday when the sunny summer breeze
> Has dried the dew and all its ropes relent,
> So that in guys it gently sways at ease,
> And its supporting central cedar pole,
> That is its pinnacle to heavenward
> And signifies the sureness of the soul,
> Seems to owe naught to any single cord,
> But strictly held by none, is loosely bound
> By countless silken ties of love and thought
> To everything on earth the compass round,
> And only by one's going slightly taut
> In the capriciousness of summer air
> Is of the slightest bondage made aware.

Two traditions

The new tent fuses the modern suspension bridge with the traditional tent, each bringing with it different ways of thinking and different spatial relationships. The former involves linear spanning to provide a passageway, and the latter is concerned with spatial envelopment using a lightweight, three-dimensional membrane. Unlike the development of the modern tent, which only began in earnest after 1952, the development of the suspension bridge coincided with the industrial revolution in England, giving it a nearly 150-year head start on the engineering experience and technology that would become the basis of contemporary tensile architecture. As the earliest paradigm of the 20th-century tensile structure, the suspension bridge encouraged such high engineering goals as strength, size and stability. Tents and shell structures, on the other hand, emphasized envelopment and shape, for which there were any number of options to choose from. The suspension bridge differs in this last respect as one suspension bridge looks much like another, each having a stiffened road deck supported from a continuous cable. With uniformly distributed loads, cables from bridge to bridge have the same classic parabolic shape. Traditional tent shelters possess greater functional flexibility and are better suited to architectural requirements. They are also essentially sculptures made out of fabric, adding to their visual interest.

It was the engineering approach, rather than anything specific or detailed, that was transferred to membrane structures. The requirements of tent design are very different to those of bridge design, and modern materials and how they were applied had to be rethought. Suspension bridge techniques were proven and reliable, but were inappropriate in terms of scale and behaviour at the architectural level. This engineering approach, which focused on strength and stiffness, differed substantially from the architectural response, which concerned itself more with achieving better shapes. The confusion between the two strands resulted in solutions that were neither one thing nor the other, but were frequently something entirely new altogether. The new tent had to find its own path, ultimately disregarding the suspension-bridge paradigm which unduly restricted the search for ever-better shapes.

The tent's essential characteristic of envelopment is self-evident and more in keeping with the architectural objective of moulding space to human activities, whereas suspension-bridge engineering was more suited to linear industrial uses (such as production lines) and large, uninterrupted spaces (such as aircraft hangars). The objective was measured in ever-longer spans. But beyond a certain point, greater spans become irrelevant in architecture where the aim is directed more towards qualitative aspects. Bridge design is directed towards simple structural objectives, and is less concerned with the synthesis of multiple objectives. At about the same time that modern tensile structures were being developed in the 1950s (and when Germany urgently needed replacements for the bridges on

[opposite] **ANZAC Bridge, Glebe Island, Sydney (Australia), 1995.**

[right] **Thomas Telford's suspension bridge over the Menai Straits (UK), 1826.**

[far right] **Clifton Suspension Bridge over the Avon Gorge, near Bristol (UK), by Isambard Kingdom Brunel, 1864.**

the Rhine that were destroyed in the closing stages of World War II), cable-stayed cantilever bridges, which were ideal on rivers of medium width, began to come into prominence. With its shorter spans, the cable-stayed system was readily adapted to architecture. The new cable-stayed bridges were particularly elegant, especially in the single-plane version, with its appealing harp-like forms making wonderful sculptural figures against the sky. They looked like skeletal diagrams of force.

The American lightweight visionary Buckminster Fuller (1895–1983) famously asked architects how much their buildings weighed. Fuller, whose US Pavilion for Expo 67 is his most admired work, insisted that architectural performance be measured against weight per pound or ton units, in the same way that ships are registered according to water displacement. He rejected style, insisting instead that buildings should be seen as economical, efficient, trouble-free machines for mass production. His polyhedra geodesic domes were used extensively to house the line radar system for the 4,500-mile Distant Early Warning line across northern Canada, but their wider application was constrained by their inflexible geometry. Fuller believed that it was the task of designers to construct efficiently in order to make the most of 'Spaceship Earth's' limited resources. A charismatic lecturer whose message is only now being fully understood, Fuller's Utopian ideas impressed many of his followers, including Frei Otto.

Though still widely used by circuses and the military, in the 1950s tents were an obscure and forgotten field of research. Otto had the field all to himself. In hindsight this is surprising, but could be explained in terms of the millions who saw service under wet canvas during World War II. Tents were undeniably efficient, lightweight and portable, but they could also be distressingly uncomfortable. With the exception of Le Corbusier, architects largely ignored them. But in many ways, tents were made to order for Modernism. After all, they fitted the Modernist programme perfectly, being prefabricated shelters that were ideally suited to off-site mass production. Why then were they neglected by

architects? The answer, most probably, was that Modernism was inspired by Cubism and Elementarism and opposed Expressionism. The machine style coincided with a cubic aesthetic, not with a complex organic sensuousness. The question is less why tents were neglected for so long, and more why they were ever developed at all. The solution really comes down to one person: Frei Otto, Fuller's natural successor. He alone took the traditional tent and gave it its modern recognizable forms. The history of lightweight architecture would have been very different and far less interesting without him.

The story of the suspension bridge is a heroic tale of daring engineering overcoming impossible odds to achieve unbelievably long spans. The Golden Gate Bridge across San Francisco Bay has become a world-famous symbol of that city, and the magnificent Brooklyn Bridge has had a great creative impact on the American imagination, inspiring painters (Georgia O'Keeffe, Joseph Stella), poets (Hart Crane) and photographers (Walker Evans). Suspension bridges were the high-fliers of engineering and, prior to man's landing on the moon, they exemplified the modern era almost as much as skyscrapers (cable-stayed bridges, with their shorter spans, have been much less celebrated). With a central span of 1,300m, the Verrazano-Narrows Bridge in New York was the world's longest in 1964. Since then it has been surpassed by the Humber Estuary Bridge (1,410m) in England and the Akashi-Kaikyo Bridge (1,990m) in Japan. Slated for completion in 2012, Italy's €3.8 billion Messina Straits suspension bridge will have a central span of 3.3km and an overall length of 5km. Its towers alone are 383m high. Suspension bridges do the job when nothing else will.

By the mid-20th century, the distinction between suspension bridges and tents, engineering and architecture, began to dissolve and the two paradigms of tensile structure merged into a combination of primary cable armature supports and secondary fabric skins. The recent history of modern tensile architecture opens with the adaptation of suspension-bridge technology and ends with the appearance of a new super-tent in the 1980s, often combining

[above] **Golden Gate Bridge, San Francisco, California (USA), 1933–37. Joseph B. Strauss and Irving Morrow, architects.**

[opposite] **The suspension bridge as building: Pier Luigi Nervi's paper mill at Burgo (Italy), 1962.**

steel cable-nets with fabric liners. In as much as the tent encloses space and the suspension bridge does not, this was, to some degree, predictable. The emergence of a more efficient, larger span and lighter tent was not inevitable and required a creative synthesis that was unusual even then. In the early 1960s, Pier Luigi Nervi designed a 148m-long paper mill at Burgo, near Mantua, with a roof suspended like the road deck of a suspension bridge. Ammann & Whitney, engineers of the Verrazano-Narrows Bridge, also engineered the cable-roof structures of the TWA and Pan Am hangars at New York's John F. Kennedy Airport, and Saarinen's hanging roof at Dulles International Airport. With its established tradition of long-span achievement, American architecture was certain to be strongly influenced by bridge engineering, whereas in Europe its influence was predictably less pronounced. Structural engineer Jörg Schlaich, the founder of Schlaich Bergermann, is typical of the engineer's approach with a professional office practice that includes the design of footbridges, large road and railway bridges, stadium roofs and futuristic solar updraft power generators. Schlaich has a unique global reputation for pushing boundaries and taking risks.

To summarize then, modern lightweight tensile architecture is the by-product of two distinct paradigms. Almost by accident, their hybridization coincided with a renewed interest in architectural space and a revolution in spatial perception. Modern architecture very nearly missed the tent entirely, and it was left to third-generation Modernists like Frei Otto to give the tent its contemporary interpretation. Whilst suspension bridges were all about engineering and metallurgy, tents extended the limits of architectural performance. Now that 'lightweight' and 'sustainable' have become the new catchwords for an ecologically responsible architecture, tents also represent the future.

Frei Otto and shapes

Like Buckminster Fuller, Frei Otto is a visionary and prophet, environmentalist, inventor, artist, architect and engineer. He did more than give the tent its modern form; he invented a series of applications and constructed a completely new ideology to go with it. Both Otto's father and grandfather were sculptors, perhaps a factor in the sculptural quality of his own structures and in his use of models and photography in preference to mathematical analysis. This artistic impulse lay at the heart of his turning to nature as an exemplary source of efficient lightweight structural paradigms. The visual and sculptural aspects of his work are integrated with structural concerns, and interact in a complex way that produced buildings of outstanding clarity. Otto was obsessed by the idea of force manifested purely as sculptural form: form follows, and is structure.

Born in 1925 at Siegmar, in Saxony, Otto was as a youth apprenticed briefly to a stonemason and learned to fly gliders. During World War II he served in a Luftwaffe fighter squadron, and after the war ended studied architecture at the Royal Polytechnic Institute of Berlin. These mixed experiences undoubtedly impressed upon Otto the significance of shape in aeronautical design. Aircraft design and tent design, though seemingly unrelated, are both exercises in discovering the most efficient, purely beautiful and nakedly

functional shapes. One of Otto's most significant innovations was iterative modelling procedures, known as 'form-finding', whereby configuring points of support and restraint generates an entirely new series of shapes, rather like mutations in biology, from which the most suitable shape is chosen. Otto effectively replaced the age-old method of sketching designs with a purely mechanical process that pointed to the most optimum structural form with a minimum surface. The beauty of this procedure was that it spontaneously integrated the aesthetic and structural considerations in a sculptural form. It was rational, yet allowed functional variation.

Even a structure as small as his peaked tent over a dance floor at the Federal Garden Show in Cologne (see p. 14) has a spare elegance that is pure art. The svelte, upswept line of the single-masted rain shelter imposes itself against the pointed outline of the cathedral on the far bank. Otto realized intuitively that tents possess a delicate explicitness, which directly exposes the flow of force. Nothing in the shape is false or hidden (Nervi called it the 'truthful style'). The patterns of overlapping seams form darker wedge strips, mapping the flow of force in the fabric. The seam pattern is explicitly structural yet decorative, both functional and art of a high order. Otto experimented with textile structures from 1952 to 1959, before moving on to pneumatic structures. After 1961, he became interested in shells, space frames with rigid joints, and suspended structures in the lead-up to *Zugbeanspruchte Konstruktionen*, his first volume on tension structures, published in 1962. This was

the beginning of his research into new shapes for tents. He was assisted by Peter Stromeyer, whose family company at Konstanz had fabricated tents for more than a century. In 1958, Otto established a studio at Zehlendorf, Berlin, which in 1964 would become the Institute for Lightweight Structures at Vaihingen, outside Stuttgart.

Otto brought the tent into the 20th century and gave it its definitive modern shape, arguably his greatest contribution. Using minimal soap-film and fabric models, he increased the range of shapes from simple, prestressed saddle surfaces to include saddle shapes between arches, and undulating and humped surfaces. At the same time, he explored the effect of different edge arrangements on such shapes. Otto isolated traits such as economy, lightness, folding, demountability, and recurring patterns, and by considering each derived new structural types. He quickly recognized the tent's minimal nature, and went on to invent the new eco-tent (assuming it had ever ceased to be that) for our time. Implicit in his structural philosophy was the rejection of anything extraneous and the insistence on structural purity, ultimately leading to ecological rigour. Tents represent a total commitment to the paradigm of structure, reduced to its absolute minimum. Whereas Buckminster Fuller had at one time seriously contemplated covering Manhattan with a transparent dome, Otto looked beyond and proposed Arctic mega-domes designed as self-contained agri-scapes. More than anyone, it was Otto who lifted the status of the tent by demonstrating that it could be efficient, beautiful and adaptable.

[above, left] The underside of a tent, showing the structural yet decorative seam pattern, Konstanz (Germany), 1955. Frei Otto, architect, with Stromeyer.

[above, right] Simple saddle surfaces.

[opposite, left] Interior of the West Germany Pavilion, Expo 67, Montreal (Canada). Frei Otto, architect.

[opposite, right] 'Snow and Rocks' Pavilion, Lausanne (Switzerland), 1963. Frei Otto, architect.

Traditional tents had been limited to a few basic shapes, from simple, conoid shapes to pyramidal and hipped-roof ones. Occasionally, as seen in the 15th-century image of *Jousting at St Inglevert*, a conoid roof might be embellished by the addition of two levels of dormers. Or, as in the case of a Bedouin black tent, the weight of the fabric causes it to hang between its pole supports so that it roughly resembles a prestressed surface. It is weight, not fabric tension, which makes the tent cloth of the Bedouin tent stable. Shape is the key to modern membrane stability. In contemporary tents, the membrane is stabilized by equal opposite forces in the doubly curved surface, and not by its weight, which is practically negligible. Simple anticlastic saddle surfaces, or some variation of them, are the basis of all new tent shapes. An early example is Otto's four-point music pavilion at Kassel in 1955. The opposite corners of its square fabric were anchored to the ground and held in the air by masts at alternate corners. The result was an opposed, doubly curved surface, which under prestress, remains stable under both upward and downward loads. The shape of a surface is determined by whether it is supported at points or along ridges or valleys. The disposition of alternating anchors and peaks or valleys and ridges that pull the fabric in opposite directions is the fundamental principle not only of fixed roofs, but also of the mobile retractable roofs that Otto designed. It largely comes down to the arrangement of the supports and anchor points.

As his structures became larger, Otto introduced cables, at first round the edges of the membrane, and then later, as at the 'Snow and Rocks' Pavilion in Lausanne, the membrane itself was reinforced by cable-nets. Four years later at Expo 67, the membrane for his West Germany Pavilion was hung under a continuous cable-net with cable eye-loop supports that distributed the net loads from each support more evenly through the net. In principle, the tent's basic shape remained the same as it had always been. Even large-scale cable-net roofs, such as those for the 1972 Olympic Games in Munich (the climax of this line of development), had flattened saddles of opposed curvature. Little has changed since then in today's new tents. Subsequent advances have been about replacing Otto's laborious physical measuring models with quicker, more effective computer programs to establish exact optimum surface shapes and cutting-patterns.

Breakthrough and beyond

One of the most exciting breakthroughs in the 1960s was the emergence of a greatly increased range of shapes and types of lightweight fabric structural applications. The choices previously available were extremely limited, and an expanded and entirely new world of possibilities now opened up, based on science that was systematic and rational. These new fabric categories in various materials included convertible or retractable roofs, grid shells covered with fabric (a development of the collapsible Mongol yurt), giant umbrellas, pneumatics, enormous air-supported greenhouses, silos, storage skins, and so on. Otto's methodical approach produced

astonishing results, and his advances seem all the more striking because the field had been neglected for so long. Constrained by tradition, tents risked being seen as irrelevant. Otto's appreciation of tents was sharpened by his experience of post-war austerity. Although it was by no means obvious at the time, ecological issues were to later assume ever-greater importance and lead inexorably to the eco-tent. One feature of membrane architecture that especially fascinated Otto was the tent's role in conditioning the environment: providing shade, trapping sunlight, or creating dams of cold air. To Otto, 'form follows function' was less a statement about aesthetic minimalism than an injunction to build economically. If contemporary architects were serious about architecture being a functional art, rather than symbolizing function, there could be no better place to start than with the tent.

In the 1960s, the British Archigram group tore a page from the Futurist manifesto of 1914, which rejected 'the sense of the monumental, of the heavy, of the static' and embraced a 'taste for the light, the practical, the ephemeral and the swift', and enlarged upon the Futurists' obsession with impermanence, speed and movement. Half a century after the appearance of the manifesto, Archigram embarked on a similar campaign of their own, which included anti-monumental pneumatic environments, walking cities and habitable capsules, in keeping with the new music scene of Swinging London. Their futuristic Pop Art vision demanded a suitably dematerialized nomadic architecture of 'elasticity and lightness'. Not much came of their cartoon proselytizing, but Archigram did succeed in shaking the architectural establishment out of its slumbering apathy and creating support for the likes of Frei Otto. Archigram made nomadism radical: the *Whole Earth Catalogue* was published, and lightweight pneumatic shelters and anything, including tents, that lay outside convention were chic. Archigram envisaged tents, balloons and Zeppelins in their fantastic leisure complexes, wrapped their Sin Centre (1961) for London's Leicester Square in transparent foil, and inserted adjustable walls inside the movable pneumatic

envelope of their 'Control and Choice' project (1967). Their anarchic version of a nomadic urbanism consisted of environments structured around mobile tents as replacements for bourgeois materialism. In 1969, Archigram's competition entry for an entertainment centre in Monaco even included the placement of electronic servicing nodes in the landscape. Life would be one long, endless rock 'n' roll party. It would take another thirty years before electronics caught up with Archigram's vision.

1972 was the year that modern tensile architecture emerged onto the world stage: the Munich Olympic Games provided Germany with the opportunity to present its new post-war democratic face. The transparent cable-net and spun-Plexiglas main stadium could not have been more different from the heavy Neoclassicism of the 1936 Games. The lightness and transparency of the Munich stadia architecture was nothing if not symbolic. It remains a watershed in modern membrane structures, separating the early experimental phase from a later, mature phase that saw the consolidation and application of the new discoveries in fabric structures. In retrospect, it is still surprising how modern the early membrane projects look today, and how little has fundamentally changed. What was previously a vigorous tributary now joined the mainstream, more architects became involved and the range of new applications grew.

Under the farsighted editorship of Monica Pidgeon, *Architectural Design* had published Frei Otto's work in the late 1960s, bringing it to the notice of students in particular and assisting in popularizing the new lightweight technology and shapes. This in turn made the task of innovative engineers such as Ted Happold and Peter Rice less difficult. For a brief moment, lightweight tensile architecture acquired a Pop Art status. Walter Bird in the US challenged the German engineering lead by using Teflon-coated fibreglass fabric for a wide range of sizeable projects, including the Pontiac Silverdome in Michigan (1975), Bullock's department store in San Jose, California (1979), a field house for the University of Riyadh, and most famously, the open-sided Haj Terminal (1981), which was constructed of 210 prefabricated fabric elements. But American structures often lacked the vital expressive element that distinguished Otto's projects; the cutting-patterns were devised to save fabric and the result tended to be less aesthetically satisfactory. The engineer was more fully in charge, and this showed. The success of the Munich stadium roofs in 1972 lifted confidence in the new tensile technology, suggesting applications far beyond anything previously achieved with traditional materials. The future was now clearly about large-scale cable-nets clad with permanent Plexiglas plate materials or the new coated fibreglass fabrics. Such developments hastened the diffusion of tensile roofs, which in turn led to new applications in stadiums, airports, exhibition centres and trade fairs.

By the 1980s, membrane structures had entered the era of the super-tent. These super-tents were not simply larger than previous fabric structures, they took tensile architecture into a new dimension using unfamiliar materials that required new design techniques to push their capabilities onto an even higher plane of performance. As well as representing the marriage between tent and suspension bridge, the super-tent also indicated the emergence of a new capable structural genre. Random factors were at work, and one of these was Frei Otto, who had provided a vision of the tent that was radically different from the past. The new generation of British membrane architects differed from the Americans and from Frei Otto in that their sense of lightweight structures was informed by the industrial revolution, which had earlier influenced James Stirling before solidifying as High Tech. It was from High Tech that the new tent architecture first showed itself in an early large roof for Norman Foster's Hammersmith Centre (1979) in London and in a shopping centre enclosure (1984) at Basildon in Essex by Michael Hopkins (see pp. 80, 84, 118 and 166), whose name was to become almost synonymous with membrane structures.

Foster and Hopkins, together with Nicholas Grimshaw (see p. 184), illustrate the British approach to membrane structures, which sees them very much as adjuncts or extensions of steel construction. The great age of engineering represented by railway stations and Joseph Paxton's Crystal Palace for the Great Exhibition of 1851 form an inescapable backdrop to British Modernism. Membrane structures and foil pillows readily slot into High Tech as a substitute for glass. This reluctance to abandon steel structure completely is typical of the way that membrane structures have been interpreted, and goes hand-in-hand with the tendency to associate membrane structures with entertainment. Distinct national approaches – styles might not be too strong a word – are evident in tensile architecture. The American approach is to regard membranes as engineering with a marginal architectural planning input, whereas the German attitude is more about achieving a synthesis that unites architecture, sculpture and pure membrane thinking. The British, partly influenced by German developments, see membrane structures through the lens of 19th-century engineering, and, for a few, by resurrecting the ghost of Italian Futurism.

New materials

The advent of new synthetic fabric materials revolutionized tent design in much the same way that the introduction of wire rope and strand had changed suspension bridge engineering a century earlier. In a fabric structure, the envelope and structure are the same thing; no other function is more critical than the structural. Unlike steel or concrete structures, which can be enlarged to support greater loads, woven fabric is a thin membrane whose strength is constrained by its thickness and number of threads per centimetre, thus setting a definite limit on practicable spans. When that limit is reached, stronger supporting nets must be introduced. Its strength not only dictates the fabric's durability, maximum span and curvature, and resistance to weathering, ultraviolet light and soiling, but also under what circumstances it can be used.

Form in architecture is generally prescribed, and the range of possible shapes is limited by the materials themselves, how they are produced, and cultural conventions and practical cost considerations. With shell structures, shape is a significant part of the structural problem since it determines the relative stiffness that can be achieved. Structure and form are the same thing; everything you see is structure, and only 1mm or so separates the outside from the inside. And since membranes are only rarely rectilinear, their shape is unusually sculptural and expressive. With all the electrical cabling, pipes, air-conditioning ducts, decorative finishes, doors and windows that must be accommodated, and so much of a building given over to hiding assorted services, architects are unaccustomed to handling such rigorous structural truth. It is impossible to hide services in tents, so ways must be found that do not conflict with or detract from the clarity of the structural form. Fabric structures must withstand two sets of loads: an initial prestress, and superimposed loads from snow, wind or construction (i.e., workers walking on the roof). The tension force in a tent cloth must be resisted by equal and opposite forces in the support masts and anchorages that withstand loads and channel them to the ground through tension. Tensile strength, in turn, depends on (or is determined by) the fibres that compose a fabric.

Textiles date back to at least 8000 BC. Flax was cultivated in Mesopotamia, Assyria and Babylon, while Egypt was famed as the 'land of linen' (fragments of Egyptian cloth have been dated to 4500 BC). Cotton, another cellulose fibre, originated in India between 3500 and 3000 BC and spread westward, reaching Assyria in 700 BC, about the same time that local bas-reliefs begin depicting tents (see p. 12). Pre-modern tents were made from animal skins (such as deer or buffalo), birch bark, felt or reed mats, or plant fibres, like hemp or cotton, which were spun into yarns and woven into canvas or duck. Lacking access to flax or cotton, ancient nomadic peoples were forced instead to use goat, camel or yak hair, or wool fibres from their flocks. Black or dark goat hair produced a coarse, open texture cloth with a low light transmission that swelled when wet, closing the fabric and making it more waterproof during inclement weather. Its openness also permitted air to circulate around the fabric threads and keep them cool in the sun, unlike today's synthetic fibres. Likewise, felt from greasy sheep's wool is a wonderful thermal insulator that repels moisture. But traditional

[right] Elevation showing the intermediate area between the stadium and gymnasium roofs, Munich (Germany), 1972. Frei Otto, architect.

woven fabrics burn easily and deteriorate relatively quickly, and the new synthetic fibres (primarily nylon, polyester and fibreglass) were pressed into service as soon as they became available. The disadvantage of the new materials, however, is that while they are undoubtedly stronger and superior in other respects, they do not respond to moisture in the same way as their ancient predecessors.

Isotropic and anisotropic membranes

The terms 'isotropic' and 'anisotropic' distinguish surfaces that have similar (isotropic) or different (anisotropic) properties in opposing (perpendicular) directions. Rubber and sheet-metal membranes, plastic sheets and fleeces are all isotropic membranes since they possess equal properties in all directions. Orthogonal woven fabrics are nearly always anisotropic, and have different properties in different directions. An anisotropic textile will exhibit different behaviour (stretch more or deform more) depending on the direction of the tension load. In woven textiles, threads are interlaced in the two perpendicular directions of warp and weft, with the warp running down the loom and the weft yarn running over and under the warp. Because the warp threads are tautly stretched, the interlaced weft threads spun around them stretch more under load. What was previously a straight line, therefore, is reconfigured like a spring and now stretches about twice the length of the straight thread.

The strength of a textile is determined by the number of filaments used in twisting the yarn thread and the yarn-count per centimetre. Tension structures commonly employ a heavier fabric with a three-ply twisting. A woven fabric will have a 'preferred' direction, whose strength is measured in terms of force (Newtons) over a 5cm-wide strip since the cross-sectional area cannot be determined. The elongation at rupture in a PVC-coated polyester fabric (such as Trevira by Hoechst) is 14 to 15 per cent in the warp direction and 20 to 23 per cent in the weft direction (roughly 50 per cent greater). Light and loosely woven fabrics undergo angular distortion, in which the orthogonal meshes distort and form diamond shapes. Such fabrics deform more

readily in three dimensions, whether synclastically or anticlastically, without or in combination with permanent elastic strains. This is a useful property. Stronger, more closely woven fabrics such as silicone-coated fibreglass will resist deformation more and suffer a greater loss of tensile strength when crimped. Organic fabrics, in general, are very extensible and even out stress redistributions more readily.

The performance of the new synthetic fibres depends very much on how they are spun into yarns, and how the yarns are woven and coated, along with the method of coating. Coatings fill the tiny spaces between the warp and weft yarns and increase the resistance of the orthogonal meshes to distortion on the diagonal, making it harder for a surface to deform in three dimensions. Consequently, a coated fabric is more prone to stress concentrations since the more easily a fabric deforms, the more easily it will shed stress to other neighbouring regions of the fabric surface. The membrane is the largest and most visible component in a fabric construction, and because it is simultaneously both structure and envelope, its other qualities (including shape) will determine its long-term appearance and functionality, along with the success of the completed structure. The correct choice of fabric, therefore, is decisive, as it will affect both performance and satisfaction afterwards. From a structural design viewpoint, fabric membranes can be treated as fine-meshed networks similar to non-rigid cable networks with square meshes, whose main difference is mesh size.

In any portion of a fabric, if the stresses along the warp and the weft are the same in the prestress condition, the material will have equal curvature in both directions. Excellent models of this minimal surface condition can be simulated with soap-film (see p. 37). Depending on their geometry, rigid boundaries such as walls, beams and arches modify the stress condition in a local fabric area. Of all the roles a fabric plays, none is more crucial than its structural function. Architectural fabrics must withstand an initial prestress load and subsequent superimposed loads, as well as the asymmetrical momentary loads caused during construction, which the masts, cables and membrane must be capable of handling without affecting fabric strength later.

New fabrics

The industrial production of high-quality fabrics today employs the most modern production processes under the most exacting standards, and, in the case of coated fabrics, is subject to certified quality controls. There are two basic types of fabrics: coated and uncoated. In uncoated fabrics that use bond types, the yarn used is twisted from filaments and then woven into the raw fabric, whereas in coated varieties, the raw fabric receives a further series of pre-treatments before being coated on both sides with vinyl PVC or silicone (in the case of polyester fabrics), or with PTFE or silicone (in the case of fibreglass fabrics). As a final process a topcoat is sometimes applied, which can be a fluorine lacquer that seals the surface (as with PVC-coated polyester fabrics) to improve its resistance to soiling, moisture and ultraviolet light. Three types of coated fabrics have accounted for 90 per cent of all membranes used in modern architectural projects: PTFE (Polytetrafluoroethylene)-coated fibreglass; PVC (Polyvinyl chloride)-coated polyester; and ETFE (Ethylene-tetrafluoroethylene)-coated foil. Every air-supported structure since the US Pavilion for Expo 70 in Osaka (see p. 8) has used fibreglass coated with PTFE (known in the US as Teflon).

PVC-coated polyester

Whereas PTFE has been used in construction since the 1970s, and transparent high-performance ETFE foil (in double- or triple-layer pneumatic constructions) only established itself in the mid-1990s, PVC-coated polyester fabric has been used for building membranes since the 1950s. In addition to these three main fabrics, there are a host of others: uncoated, open materials; micro-perforated membranes with good acoustic absorbency values; uncoated or impregnated, narrow- or broad-weave fabrics for internal applications; polyester fabrics with low flammability coatings internally; low-emissivity (low-E) glass fabrics with fluoropolymer coating

and an acoustic absorbent structure. Architectural fabrics are a highly specialized field. Frequently, the choice of a fabric will come down to either a PVC-coated polyester or PTFE-coated fibreglass, with PVC-coated polyester being the most commonly used for membrane structures. It is possible to produce PVC-coated polyester fabrics that have a resistance of 1,000kp/5cm and over, but normally it is sufficient to have resistances of 300 to 600kp/5cm and thicknesses of 0.7mm to 1.2mm. Such a relatively thin material has little heat insulation, but can be made non-inflammable and cold resistant. PVC-coated polyester costs about half that of PTFE fibreglass, but is inherently less durable.

PVC-coated polyester fabric is more suitable for demountable structures, which are folded and transported or stored, than fibreglass. Frei Otto chose it for the sports complex at King Abdul Aziz University in Jeddah because it provided a more flexible exterior skin and was less prone to damage during handling than PTFE-coated fibreglass. Over time, the plasticizers in the vinyl rise to the surface, creating a sticky base to which dust, dirt and mildew can adhere. It must be cleaned regularly if painted with urethane, or laminated with a more durable membrane. By contrast Skidmore, Owings & Merrill's Haj Terminal is the 20th-century equivalent of the Crystal Palace, requiring 510,950m² of PTFE-coated fibreglass fabric. The specific material characteristics were determined by the weaving and the coating; the fibre was woven by Chemfab from Owens Corning's Beta fibreglass, and coated by passing it through a vat of milky Teflon by DuPont.

Service life is determined by many factors; translucent materials can be guaranteed to last twelve years and opaque ones up to twenty years. Coated fabrics need practically no maintenance and are relatively easy to change later. White is the best colour because it reduces surface temperatures, thus increasing the fabric's service life. The more transparent a fabric is, the shorter its service life will be. Polyester yarn and soft PVC compounds show practically no signs of rotting. One of the most impressive early applications of PVC-coated polyester was the West Germany

[opposite] **An ETFE pillow is placed between the lines of domes in the roof. Southern Cross (formerly Spencer Street) Station, Melbourne (Australia), 2006. Nicholas Grimshaw, architect.**

Pavilion for Expo 67 in Montreal. It had a total roof surface of 8,500m² that weighed only 6,100kg (0.72kg/m²), and at the time was the largest building of its type in the world.

PTFE-coated fibreglass

Although PVC-coated polyester and PTFE-coated fibreglass are of similar tensile strength, there are important differences. The latter is much more expensive, and has both a lower degree of elasticity and a poor flexing behaviour that results in cracking and self-abrasion of the coating. Furthermore, it makes greater demands on the detailing of the connections, fabrication and installations, and, to a degree, on the structural design of the substructure. But PTFE-coated fibreglass is superior in terms of its durability (more than twenty-five years, rather than twelve or twenty years), long-term appearance, resistance to chemicals, superior fire rating, resistance to ultraviolet light, and light reflectance.

Alternative coatings can be applied to fibreglass fabrics such as fluoropolymer, which allow a considerable range of translucency varying from 0 to 50 per cent. PTFE-coated fibreglass can also be printed. A great advance in recent years is a highly translucent product made on a PTFE basis that is foldable and, unlike most fibreglass fabrics, can be welded and made rainproof by giving it a special coating. Silicone-coated fibreglass fabric, an inexpensive alternative to PTFE-coated fibreglass with an equivalent fire rating, has not made the jump to exterior use because it soils easily.

ETFE-coated foil

ETFE is at present the most widely used foil. THV foil is only suitable for small spans because it is less tear resistant, and PVC foil is used for small to medium spans in interiors and for temporary uses. The brilliant Eden Project in Cornwall (p. 184), completed in 2001, made ETFE foil-covered cushions on giant 'bubble' space frames instantly recognizable around the globe. Since then, foil pillows have been incorporated into such high-profile projects as Grimshaw's National Space Centre at Leicester and PTW Architects' 'Water Cube' swimming stadium for

the Beijing Olympic Games in 2008 (p. 190). The technology is still new, thus giving ETFE a reputation as a futuristic space-age material.

Foil pillows are small, two- and three-layer tensile structures with spans of up to 3.5m to 4.5m in one direction. The foil is framed around the edge by aluminium perimeter extrusions that are supported by a primary load-bearing building structure. The geometrical flexibility of the pillows and lighter support-structure weight results in overall financial and energy savings. They are also a practical choice for low-mass convertible roofs. ETFE pneumatic pillows can have from two up to five layers of 90 to 150 micron thin foil inflated to a slight excess pressure of 200Pa to 1,000Pa for structural stability. It has a lower load-bearing strength than woven fabric. Pillow beams can be formed up to 30m long. The foil is manufactured in sheets up to 250μ, with a maximum width of 1.55m. To improve thermal insulation, a stretched intermediate layer, which has no load-bearing function, can be added to pneumatic wall and roof units to increase the U-value to 2.0W/m²K.

Chemically inert ETFE foil is unaffected by ultraviolet light and atmospheric pollution. Because it weighs only 2 to 3.5kg/m², ETFE foil permits greater spans than glass, has an anticipated life in excess of forty years, and can be used as a specialized replacement for glass. ETFE foil is a fully recyclable material with a self-cleaning surface that can be printed upon to vary its reflectivity properties. It can also be rendered translucent by incorporating a white body tint, and the translucency manipulated by pressurizing individual air chambers between layers so that the opaque graphics printed on one layer cover or uncover another. In a similar fashion, the pillows can be configured to change colour, as seen to great effect at the Allianz Arena in Munich (p. 130). Foil pillow systems, however, require years of experience for the detailed design, fabrication and fitting to be successful.

Advances continue to be made in newer, stronger fibre materials, such as Spectra 900, which is ten times stronger than steel and light enough to float. Kevlar yarns are being used in the manufacture of laminated racing mainsails for yachts, with the yarns laid along the known lines to produce a sail as a single piece with the optimum flying shape. This has resulted in sails that are 33 per cent lighter than conventional ones and that stand up to every test for wear and tear. The application of such sail technology is limited by the high cost of the mould and sizes less than 3,300m^2, but where a large number of identical membranes are required this approach could offer a significant advantage.

Metal fabrics

Ancient and medieval textiles could be sumptuous, woven through with gold and silver thread, and invading armies would melt down tons of the cloth for its precious metals. Thin, drawn gold wire was used in Italian brocaded velvets in the 15th century, and Venice was famous for its *drap d'or*, with the background woven in gold thread. So luxurious were the encampment tents at the meeting of Francis I and Henry VIII outside Calais in 1520 that the site was afterwards referred to as the Field of the Cloth of Gold. The woven metal fabrics of today are less exotic and consist in the main of round, flat or stranded wires, or cables in stainless, titanium, chromium or chromium nickel steel. Metallic filaments offer greater permanence and lustre in comparison to traditional organic or synthetic fibres. Woven metal fabrics fill a variety of uses, including sunshades on building façades, soffits and aviaries, and for electromagnetic or security protection.

In collaboration with German manufacturer GDK, architect Dominique Perrault designed and developed long sheets of metal fabric that he draped as semi-solid ceilings in the Bibliothèque Nationale (1989–95) in Paris. The engineering school in Marne-la-Vallée (1987), near Paris, is earlier, but it is at the Bibliothèque Nationale that the result is most spectacular. Here, Perrault transformed the interior into a metaphysical landscape with ten different meshes and more than 30,000m^2 of freely sculptured fabric hung wall to wall, floor to ceiling. All of this was achieved with exceptional economy, implementation, durability, maintenance and life cycle. Perrault recognized in stainless-steel fabric a spectacular

new tent material that was permanent and strong, yet flexible and capable of being formed into virtually any shape imaginable.

Solar integrated membranes

The functional characteristics of fabric have recently been extended to create new possibilities. Textile architecture can act as a filter, modifying undesirable qualities of an environment, and tent cloth, instead of merely blocking sunlight, can also generate electrical currents. In 1998, FTL/Happold designed a pavilion for an exhibition at New York's Cooper-Hewitt using the first fabric to incorporate flexible, thin-film photovoltaic panels laminated to a translucent, woven PVC-coated polyester cloth. Two years later, Martin Wolf of Solomon Cordwell Buenz & Associates won the Department of Energy's Sun Wall competition with his proposal for a concave sweep of solar panels, supported by tension trusses between the existing 2,973m^2 south-facing wall of their headquarters in Washington, DC. A photovoltaic array on the lower two-thirds of the wall would have produced electricity for air-conditioning from the more vertical summer sunlight, while above, solar panels would capture the horizontal rays of the winter sun. A pool out front cooled the air in summer to avoid superheating behind this enormous solar wall.

In Australia, Gavin Tulloch of Sustainable Technologies International went one step further by developing solar panels that could be placed on a tent and begin producing electricity immediately. Such solar panels could be used by soldiers while on reconnaissance; at present, a single soldier consumes something like 4kg of spent lithium batteries for each week in the field. The establishment in 2005 of the world's first automated production of solar integrated roofing membranes in Los Angeles by coating manufacturer Coatema marks a highly significant development in using membranes to generate electricity. On a 3m roll of PVC, 290 photovoltaic modules can realize 116kW-h. New flexible, amorphous silicone Unisolar cells are covered on top by a PTFE/ETFE membrane for protection and self-cleaning between a polyethylene-laminated base. Six flexible photovoltaic modules are parallel and continuous hot-melt laminated to a 3m-wide roofing membrane.

Photonic textiles

Further developments promise to expand the potential of the new tent. At the 2005 consumer electronics trade fair in Berlin, a team led by Martijn Kraus of Royal Philips Electronics in the Netherlands unveiled fabrics that incorporated LEDs into clothing without compromising material softness or flexibility. The light emitted from the LEDs was augmented by using shiny fabrics without overcrowding the cloth with them. The photonics could be made interactive by incorporating sensors and wireless communication technologies, such as Bluetooth. Kraus's prototype devices were powered by ordinary AA batteries, but the researchers are developing wearable, foldable batteries that recharge with movement.

A problem with all lightweight structures (and a particular problem at the 1972 Munich Olympic Games) is the intrusiveness of bulky electric lighting and air-conditioning. But photonic textiles could eliminate these irritating necessities by making the tent fabric a photonic medium. Photonic textiles have a wide range of applications in fashion, safety gear, ski apparel and directional lighting on carpets. In applications such as sports arenas that require high-intensity lighting, photonic textiles will probably not replace existing technology, but when they are introduced some time after 2007, and where a diffuse ambient light is suitable, they promise a new era in the development of the new tent.

The traditional tent has been transformed by stronger and longer-lasting fabric materials in combination with new, more effective structural shapes. And this truly modern adventure is not

Standard Membrane Material Properties

Properties	PVC-coated polyester fabric	PTFE-coated fibreglass fabric	ETFE fluoropolymer foil
Cost £ *(March 2005)*	£150–400/m²	£300–550/m²	£550–750/m²
Cost € *(November 2004)*	€15–15/m²	€150–230/m²	€300/m²
Weight	0.6–1.65kg/m²	0.4–1.6kg/m²	0.4–1.6kg/m²
Tensile strength	2,000–10,000N/5cm	1,000–8,000N/5cm	1,000–5,000N/5cm
Light transmission	0–25 per cent	4–22 per cent	94–97 per cent
Light reflectance	50–70 per cent	65–75 per cent	60 per cent
UV light resistant	Good	Excellent	Excellent
Colours	White, can be pigmented to any standard colour, non-white colours reduce lifespan	Typically white, some metallized fabrics available	Can be overprinted with a variety of surfaces to affect transmission, or printed with graphic patterns to reduce solar gain
Joining	Stitching or welding	Pressure heat sealing	Bonding or fusing smooth surface
Durability	15–20 years	+ 25–30 years	+ 40 years
Self-cleaning property	Generally good	Excellent	Excellent
Acoustics	Very transparent	Very transparent	Relatively transparent
Resistance to chemicals	Good	Excellent	Inert
Handling	Easy to fold	Critical	Critical
Recyclable	Good	Neutral	Excellent
Fire rating	Low	Non-combustible	Non-combustible
Insulating value U	2.6W/m²K for two layers with 200mm air gap	4.6W/m²K	1.96W/m²K

over yet. Membrane architecture continues to throw up new surprises, and more are in store. Much that we are witnessing today is simply an amplification of what the tent already was, a development of its traditional features to make it even more revolutionary than ever before. The intrinsic flexibility and efficiency of fabric structures continue to keep tents alive, dynamic and relevant.

Finding a shape

In 1966, Jørn Utzon exhibited a large model of the glass walls at the open ends of the Sydney Opera House roof vaults. Strings had been stretched horizontally and vertically across them to form a flat, saddle surface in an attempt to find a suitable geometry for the structural mullions and glass. Utzon had inadvertently stumbled upon the classic anticlastic shape. Australian architect Peter Hall, who replaced Utzon on the project, substituted an a priori surface derived partly from a cone at the bottom and a cylinder above the cone. Instead of Utzon's graceful, hanging gull-wing profile or the string saddle surface, Hall imposed the current awkward glass walls. And in place of Utzon's subtle sculpture of hinged plywood, Hall's solution looks preconceived and forced. His failure provides an important lesson about form-finding: the need to solve shapes organically. The great 20th-century advance in tent design was to replace presumptive shapes with rationally determined structural criteria, and to employ modelling techniques that automatically discover the most optimal shapes for membrane structures. Consequently the structures became much more interesting and experimental when form-finding became an established procedure.

The stability of a membrane structure is shape-dependent. The more highly curved it is, the better able it will be to resist wind- and snow-loads. In textile structures, the prestress force is proportional to the radius of curvature: the smaller the radius, the lower the stress, with a maximum span of around 20m for most fabrics. This is not only structurally significant, it also adds considerably to the sculptural impact and tactile appeal. The process of form-finding involves the designer playing with a shape by shifting anchorages and supports and observing the effects. The principles really are quite simple, and the range of shapes more limited than one might initially assume. Once the constraints are accepted, form-finding can become a wonderfully exciting adventure.

Discovering a shape that satisfies all design criteria requires a holistic approach, and working with models is an excellent way for a designer to explore possibilities. Afterwards, it is relatively easy to pick which shape is satisfactory structurally and to examine concerns regarding aesthetic and planning criteria. It is simply a matter of working through the various requirements and testing them against the shapes being explored. Many of the greatest names in modern architecture used models to determine and refine their designs, either in preference to or in parallel with drawings; membrane models are a more precise extension of this architectural practice. The term 'form-finding', coined by Frei Otto, is particularly apt as it implies a search for the most optimal form.

Physical models

A wide variety of complex forms can be explored with physical models (despite lacking the accuracy of, for instance, numerical models, necessary to determine the precise prestress and surface geometry for the fabrication and stressing of surface structures), and before the advent of personal computers physical models were the only practical design tools. The type of physical models used depends on the structure. In prestressed textile surfaces, models made from soap-film, fabric and occasionally plaster were customary, but in pneumatic structures elastic membranes distended by plaster were more suitable. In his research into suspended structures and inverted grid shells, Otto suspended gold chain-nets and photographed their side-lit profiles against black backgrounds to create striking, jewel-like images of the hanging shapes. The limits of physical modelling were reached with Otto's cable-net roofs for the Munich Olympics, notably the Western Athletics Stadium, which had spans of up to 45m and up to sixty meshes. He had employed an elaborate

[opposite, top] Suspended model of a chain-net, with interior suspension points. Institute for Lightweight Structures, Vaihingen (Germany), 1971–73.

[opposite, middle] Tulle model of the final proposal for the roofs for the 1972 Olympic Games.

[opposite, below] Institute for Lightweight Structures, Vaihingen (Germany), 1968. Frei Otto, architect.

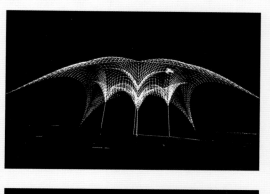

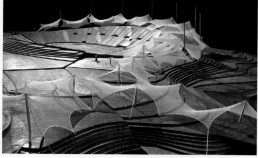

range of models, including soap-film and tulle fabric models, which he used to generate shapes and obtain reliable cutting-pattern information. Large, meticulously constructed 1:10-scale wire measuring models were eventually developed for the Olympic roofs in the search for greater precision.

A stretched membrane's stability depends on equal tension throughout the surface; nowhere can it be subject to compression forces. The presence of wrinkles or creases will indicate a soft spot in the surface where the prestress is low. Less tension is required in a highly curved surface than in a flat, less curved one. Playing with the position of masts and anchor points and adjusting the edge profile changes the distribution of stresses and helps to equalize the tension forces in a surface. Models force designers to think creatively about shape, interior space, visual patterns and the overall surface terrain. It was rumoured that Otto's roof for the West Germany Pavilion for Expo 67 controversially mirrored the combined landform of the two separate German states!

Soap-film models

A soap-film model simulates a membrane with a uniform prestress in the two orthogonal directions of 1:1 throughout. Its surface has a minimal area within the boundary condition. Many of the shapes from soap-film models are extremely elegant. But there is no reason why uniform stress membranes should be considered as superior to surfaces with variable-stress surfaces. The stress in most membrane structures will vary

since, in practice, it is often impractical to achieve uniform stress over the entire surface. Small-radius, highly curved surfaces resist wind- and snow-loads better than flatter surfaces. Depending on which is greater, the prestress ratio may be adjusted to optimize the stresses under load by increasing the curvature with associate uplift and decreasing it for download. Ponding can occur where the surface curvature is inadequate, especially at the edges. It can be very dangerous and should be avoided. Occasionally planning may dictate minimum headroom, and if this produces flat areas can lead to the formation of ponds under snow-loads.

Tulle and wire models

After exploring shapes with soap-film models, the next stage in the form-finding process is the tulle or wire model. The technical sophistication of such models increased markedly when Frei Otto began his research, and reached its climax with the structural design of the roofs for the Munich Olympics. It was at this point that a mathematical approach was adopted in the quest for greater precision.

In a prestressed membrane, the surface geometry is established for a prestress condition. Compensated strip patterns are used for cutting. The cutting-pattern for a membrane is used to establish the smaller, 'at rest' shape, which when prestressed connects with the holding or system points. Small, longitudinal errors are identical to extension errors, and equate to large strength errors. There is, therefore, a greater requirement for accuracy in the manufacture of all structural components, including the foundations and system points, as well as in the actual assembly of the net or membrane, than in any other type of construction. Even comparatively small inaccuracies in measuring have a very large effect on the prestress force. The less extensible the material is, the smaller the extension needed to achieve the required prestress, hence the criticality of the dimensioning of the roof pattern.

For the Munich roofs, Otto's team made 1:125-scale models out of spring steel wire under a predetermined tension in order to simulate the net cable. A 5cm error in the actual structure

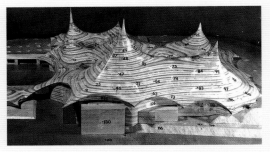

corresponded to a mesh error of 0.007mm in the model. In order to achieve greater precision, it was decided that a purely numerical approach was needed. A year-long project with John Argyris and his colleagues at the Institute of Statics and Dynamics of Aerospace Structures in Stuttgart was duly undertaken, and the results were applied to the roofs using procedures that computed with absolute accuracy the geometry of the cable-net roof.

Wind-load models

Wind- and snow-loads are important design factors. Many tensile buildings are located in regions such as Saudi Arabia, Australia and Malaysia where snow can be eliminated as a load factor, but wind is a major threat to light membrane structures. The varying intensity of wind-loads on the surface, and the performance with regard to wind, is critical in setting the prestress needed for stability. In the 1970s I observed the destruction of a circus big top during a sudden storm while the tent cloth was being raised. Successive wind gusts lifted and shook the canvas violently until a tear appeared and spread rapidly, until within a short time 50 per cent of the canvas was shredded. The failure, while not dangerous, was extremely rapid.

In the course of designing the West Germany Pavilion, wind-tunnel tests were carried out at the Institute of Aerodynamics and Gas Dynamics at the University of Stuttgart. An experimental model at a scale of 1:50 was constructed from layers of plywood in such a manner that the pressure manometer could be readily connected by means of plastic tubing to 129 pressure-test borings in the interior cavity, which were used as measuring points; fifteen of these were on the vertical enclosing walls behind the tent walls. The shape used was the undeformed surface. The model was coated in a mixture of carbon black and petroleum and exposed to the flow, and the flow-lines were observed using film attached to the model surface. Negative suction pressures predominated and the results were expressed graphically. It was found that the maximum pressures arose at the fifteen pressure-test holes located on the vertical walls. Similarly, Horst Berger carried out wind-tunnel testing on nine conoid fabric roof units at the Haj Terminal in Jeddah to establish the membrane wind-loading and flow behaviour of the large, conoid PTFE-coated fibreglass membrane modules.

Numerical models

Before the computer era, form-finding was carried out using the physical models described above to determine the geometry of a membrane shape. Today, a better result can be achieved more easily with computer software, and much actual design can now be accomplished quickly and more economically. Whilst such technological advances have made form-finding more precise and facilitated analysis, physical models still have their uses at the conceptual design stage. And in some cases, such as Otto's Mannheim grid shell (1975) where the complexity was considerable, it is debatable whether computers are in fact better than an actual model. Physical models are indispensable in assessing three-dimensional shapes, but once the basic form-finding stage is complete, load analysis and patterning can be performed solely by computers.

Although speeding up the form-finding process and making it easier to understand and analyze stress distribution, where computers are less effective is in evaluating a structure's interior spatial qualities and human appropriateness. A fingertip placed on a stretched tulle surface is often all that is needed to detect areas of under-stress, high tension and wrinkles. Physical models enable a designer to assess a shape structurally, architecturally, spatially and visually, all at once, and no computer graphic, however, sophisticated, can really tell a designer what to expect in terms of light and shadow effects, transparency and views to the outside. At this early stage, it is comparatively easy to adjust and correct the surface by moving a mast location or ground anchorage. Physical models still represent a valuable design tool, whereas computer programs offer engineers a new and powerful analytical tool that makes the task of finding the precise cutting-pattern that much surer. The two are not so much rivals as complementary methods.

None of the techniques of physical modelling can match numerical modelling in accuracy for the information required to fabricate and stress the membrane, and the advent of less extensible PTFE-coated fibreglass cloth has made the calculation of stress and cutting-pattern even more critical. With the more extensible polyester fabrics, errors are evened out. New materials (such as coated fibreglass), which are significantly stiffer than other commonly used membranes, require greater precision for pattern-making or patterning. Numerical modelling, the development of algorithms for defining the geometry of prestressed surfaces, is indispensable in the wider exploitation of tensile membrane structures, particularly at a larger scale. In the US, the first computer-patterned membrane was the roof for the Minneapolis Metrodome (1982), by Birdair. The leading fabricators in the membrane industry (including Taiyo, Birdair, Skyspan and Hightex, along with consultants Arup & Associates and Geiger Engineers) have all developed their own special software systems, tailored to suit their needs and fabrication practices. Birdair employs a matrix analysis algorithm for form-finding, in which the elements are given a very low mechanical striffness and a prescribed prestress. The equilibrium geometry is determined in an iterative analysis of the structure.

Computer-based numerical modelling of membrane structures relies on the method of finite elements. Points or nodes locate coordinates on a surface, and further node points are placed at either end of beams and masts, with cables represented by line elements at intermediate points in their length and by points on the surface. These nodes are then interconnected by a network of finite elements. Cables and beams are represented by line elements with two nodes; fabric is modelled by triangular elements, each with three connecting nodes. The forces associated with an element, such as cable tension or fabric stress, are translated into component forces at the nodes. For a structure to be in equilibrium, the sum of all forces at each node (comprising the contributions from all attached elements and any external loading) must balance out to zero in all directions. Data from form-finding (comprised of connectivity, nodal geometry and the element) constitutes the complete model description of a membrane structure and the element properties. The resultant shape can then be utilized directly for analysis. An analysis of the complete structural system is made possible by feeding in spatial data of further elements, such as struts and beams, to the shape model.

Software selection

An understanding of the capabilities and shortcomings of the different computer software used in engineering analysis is helpful in understanding the significance of the information that is produced. To start, an idealized numerical model of the structure is established from a library of standard parts so that a study of its response to varying load conditions can be made. It is important that the functional, aesthetic and structural requirements (rather than the limitations of the software) are allowed to control the design. To this end, a full range of surface stress controls for a uniform and constant stress field are used at the later form-finding stage. The engineer needs to have a clear understanding of the software, including how the algorithm will respond when, for instance, a local region of the structure is unstable due to element collapse or

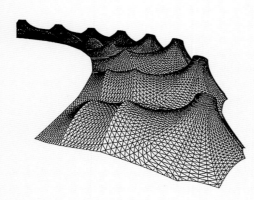

physically inadmissible controls. The reading of a structure's behaviour is aided if the analysis is based on a clear physical analogy. The constrained conditions and applied loading used, as well as any inherent approximations, also need to be understood.

Since tension structures, small or large, are non-linear systems, it is imperative that the designer fully comprehends and anticipates their behaviour under all the relevant loading conditions, and does not rely exclusively on what emerges from the 'black-box' software. There are two approaches: matrix and vector methods. The final choice of method should rest with the design engineer, and should be one he understands and is most comfortable using within the selected criteria. As computer power increases, the overall efficiency of each solution method becomes less and less important. The most important consideration, whatever the method, is that it should contribute positively to an integrated design process.

The dynamic relaxation method

Of all the vector-based methods, the dynamic relaxation method is the most widely used and efficient for form-finding and analysis because it deals flexibly and naturally with large deformations. It serves as the basis for a number of individual programs, and lends itself to the introduction of specialized elements, loading conditions and nodal constraints. It was originally perceived as a step-by-step solution, introducing small increments of force to the structure subject to viscous damping. While this may appear to be an unnecessarily roundabout approach, when applied to tension structures it offers significant advantages. It was created in the early 1970s by Alistair Day to analyze concrete nuclear containment vessels for UK construction firm Taylor Woodrow because computers at the time were not powerful enough to assemble all the matrices involved and invert them, and has been the standard ever since. At present, the University of California at Berkeley's DYNA program is the highest incarnation of the dynamic relaxation method.

The dynamic relaxation method was originally devised to study non-linear structures, which differ from linear structures in two ways: they suffer significant changes to their shape under load, and, importantly, the relationship of stress to strain is non-linear, unlike ordinary structures which are analyzed by the matrix method. In the dynamic relaxation method, the structure is modelled as a series of nodes and connecting elements, and each node is allocated a mass (in a static analysis, the result is independent of the mass). In the first cycle, the mass is initially stationary. At the end of a finite time interval, the velocity is computed and the distance travelled is equal to the average velocity multiplied by the time. This establishes the new node position. Using the stress–strain relationship, each strain in an element is converted into a stress and the sum of the stresses at each node computed as discrete forces. This calculation yields an out-of-balance resultant force referred to as the 'residual force'. This is repeated over and over until the residual force is so small as to be negligible. The acceleration is worked out using Newton's second law of motion: $F = ma$ (force equals acceleration produced by the force multiplied by the mass of the body). To stop the oscillation, the node is moved in the same direction by, for example, 95 per cent less than previous. The amount of damping is irrelevant to the actual answer, but it does affect the computing time. There are various schema to make this happen more quickly, from the mass selected to how the damping is managed.

Each cycle begins by using the current geometry to look at the stress based on the current strain. The sum of the strains gives the deformed shape, the stress in each element and the reaction force in all the supports: all the things a designer needs to know. The accuracy of the finite-element model is proportional to the number of elements modelled in the surface. How many nodes are used will depend on the accuracy that is required against the size and complexity of the model; the larger and more complex the structure, the greater the number of nodes. With upwards of 3,000 nodes, computers are essential to carry out the complex simultaneous computations involved. The final form must satisfy a range of requirements, from aesthetics to engineering performance and suitability to function, and demands a high degree of cooperation between architect and engineer. Outstanding membrane structures do not happen by accident, they are the products of a close collaborative partnership.

Form-finding

In form-finding, the designer searches for a shaped surface that will hold a uniform prestress in the two directions of a woven fabric. A membrane requires either a uniform or smoothly varied distribution of stress within the warp and weft directions of the fibres for a satisfactory long-term result. Since the shape of a membrane is determined by the geometry of its edges and the distribution of prestress within the surface, deciding on the edge geometry can be quite critical. Problems in the surface can be quickly eliminated by adjustments to the edge geometry, or by varying the location of the interior supports. Normally, a steel ring, arch or concrete perimeter beam contains the membrane, but where the membrane is lifted off the ground it is customary to use a relatively stiff cable. In the dynamic relaxation method, a particular stress–strain relationship is assumed for the material: regardless of the strain, the stress is constant. Before computers this was done using soap-film models. For a curve of constant radius, tension equals pressure multiplied by radius; the greater the radius, the greater the tension in the membrane surface. Form-finding involves finding a surface that fulfils that condition in all places.

The alignment of the fibres should ideally coincide with the directions of the principal curvature of the membrane surface. In a simple conic surface, the warp will be in a radial pattern; for a four-point saddle or hyperbolic paraboloid surface, the warp will usually connect the high-point-to-high-point seam profile in order to maximize stiffness. The surface shape is affected by the local ratios of warp-to-weft stress. In the finite-element method, warp and weft prestress values are given to the individual membrane elements, and the connecting node forces are a function of these set prestresses and the geometry. The stress fluctuates as the geometry changes until an equilibrium form is achieved. The shape is recorded using geodesic lines running from boundary to boundary, which follow the minimum distance across the surface with individual element warp directions set parallel to the neighbouring geodesic direction, and the weft directions set perpendicular. In nearly every instance, finding a shape that functions correctly and is adequate structurally depends on maintaining a radius less than 20m. It is only in large structures that this becomes a challenge. A surface radius that exceeds 20m can be reduced by introducing additional interior points of support. Unlike concrete or steel buildings that can be made larger and larger, structures made from fabric, which has a maximum thickness of approximately 1mm, are not scalable in the same way. For the roofs at the 1972 Olympics, Frei Otto overcame this limitation by introducing cable-nets that could be made larger by increasing the diameter and strength of the steel cables.

The magnitude of snow- and wind-loads is customarily set by industry design codes, and wind-tunnel tests may be demanded for large or complex structures. In some countries, snow-loading may not be applicable and this will duly affect the upward counter prestress needed to restore equilibrium. Critical points that need special attention are those of maximum stress, areas of large deflections and potential ponding, and slack areas where bidirectional wrinkling is most likely to occur. Loading is applied as vertical for snow, or at right angles to the surface for wind loads. The self-weight of the membrane is usually included in the load analysis, but because it is small it has a negligible bearing on the outcome. Of greater importance are the weights of all the active support elements. Earthquake-loading can be ignored because of the low mass and high flexibility of membrane structures.

Cutting-pattern and fabrication of panels

After form-finding, the next step is to establish the cutting-pattern for the fabric panels. With the shape established, it is now possible to analyze its behaviour under a range of loads. What is needed is the optimal way to cut the fabric from a standard roll based on two considerations: the width of fabric and how to economize the quantity of fabric required. PVC-coated polyester comes in widths of 2m, and PTFE-coated fibreglass in widths of 3m. In practice, any greater width would present a problem in achieving the required curvature since the aim is to create a curved surface from flat material.

To fabricate a membrane, individual panels are cut from rolls of fabric of standard width. Cutting-patterns are generated directly from the form model. The doubly curved surface must be transferred to a flat one, which is not stretched under an applied prestress force. Cutting-patterns are a two-dimensional approximation to a material obtained from a three-dimensional surface. The problem is analogous to transferring the spherical shape of a globe onto the flat page of an atlas, which is achieved by unfolding a set of sequential triangular finite elements onto a plane. It is customary to lay out the pattern on the fabric with the principal stress aligned with the warp direction. To ensure that the geodesic seam lines of the membrane surface do not fall outside the usable width of the fabric strip, the three-dimensional geometry of a panel must be flattened out by unfolding the triangular elements between the adjacent warp lines. When the array of diagonals between the panel nodes is reversed, the shape will be different. This disparity is handled by averaging the two, resulting in a curved, twisted surface.

The unfolded pattern represents the final stressed geometry, which must now be compensated to allow for the stretching of the material from the unstressed, as-cut state to the stressed, installed condition. Next, the unfolded compensated patterns must be presented in a format suitable for fabrication. In the past, schedules were issued which listed sets of coordinates around the boundary of each panel, but this practice has been replaced by plotting and cutting machines to minimize errors. The next step will normally occur after the structure has been tendered: a sample of the actual fabric is stretched to discover how much it will expand in both directions to achieve the required prestress, giving the strain needed to achieve the specified prestress. Once this is known, the dimensions of the panel are shrunk by that amount of strain to give the final cutting-pattern dimensions. Prefabricated in factories under strictly controlled conditions to ensure rigorous quality control, the assembled membrane panels are packed and shipped to the site for erection. To guarantee the geometrical compatibility of a membrane and the various structural supports on-site, all dimensions of the membrane elements must be derived from the same computer model.

Numerical modelling has transformed the form-finding routine in membrane structures. Because analysis has become so much easier, the imaginative and inventive aspects have become less of an adventure and more of a routine. Few engineers, with the exception of David Wakefield, the founder of Tensys, have dedicated themselves exclusively to fabric structures. Engineers often come into the industry only to develop other interests later on. Architects need to be wary of fabric salespersons who loudly proclaim freedom of shape. In practice, the range of shapes is limited in both scale and surface geometry, and architects would be wise to recognize these limits before pushing their engineers to achieve impossible shapes. Tent structures are no different from conventional architecture, so much depends on knowing the medium and respecting the innate character of woven fabric. Achieving a stable shape is not enough. The architect should feel the tension on a surface and grasp its underlying lyricism and clarity of form. Nicholas Grimshaw's Eden Project (p. 184) in Cornwall is a spectacular illustration of what can result when technology and architectural vision fuse expressively.

Realization

Eugene Freyssinet said that 'prestressing is a state of mind', and few examples illustrate this better than the black tent of Central Algeria, whose heavy cloth is lifted and automatically prestressed by drawing the two legs of the central scissor-mast closer together. The scissor-mast is both effective and simple because prestressing has been integrated into its design; in 1980,

[opposite] **The author's structure for the Frei Otto exhibition in Sydney (Australia), 1980. The net was prestressed by drawing the aluminium mast feet close together.**

I employed a similar aluminium scissor-mast in an exhibition devoted to Frei Otto. Prestress in tent membranes is required to avoid both the formation of slack areas, which look unsightly, and concerns about the membrane's dynamic behaviour should they occur. If the membrane does go slack in the wind and moves excessively, cracking can occur, especially in a brittle fabric such as PTFE-coated fibreglass.

A fabric is prestressed until the curvature in the warp and weft yarns is the same. The yarn starts out more circular, but flattens under loading. The natural looseness in a fabric must be removed to ensure that it behaves properly by overcoming fabric crimp. The amount of prestress force introduced into a fabric is fairly arbitrary, and is becoming less as engineers become more courageous. As a consequence of linear theory, engineers seek to make their structures as rigid as possible, but non-linear structures respond better to load the more flexible they are, not the reverse. The magnitude of a force is determined by the radius of curvature; the more relaxed a membrane is, the more readily it can adopt shapes of lower radius, helping to reduce the magnitude of stress (this is why sailors let the sheets off in a storm).

The erection and detailing of fabric structures is often the most testing stage. It is important to watch that both the stress and deformation behaviour, in conjunction with the determination of the construction details, is intimately linked to and assists the means used to prestress in the structure. Much like the hoisting of circus big tops up the kingpost from a head pulley, flying-masts can be positioned so they can be jacked and straight edges pulled into a more curved, scalloped cable edge to produce a closed framework. In modern tensile structures, just as in traditional tents, toggle elements at edge-cable cusp points can be shortened. Whatever the method chosen, the designer needs to consider a suitable means of applying force to the membrane that will give it an even prestress throughout. This can be achieved at the boundary or at points within the surface; the more numerous these points are, the less difficult it will be to ensure an even level of prestress and monitoring, step-by-step, of the intensification of forces. The flexibility and deformability of fabric structures calls for different thinking when it comes to details. In large membrane structures, special steel castings that allow potential freedom of movement about three axes, as well as changes on component length, will often need to be purpose-built.

The disposal of rainwater is a factor the architect ignores at his or her peril. The principal cause of failure in fabric structures around the world is the lack of drainage caused by pooling on the fabric (ponding), usually near the edge. This is especially dangerous when snow builds up and melts during the daytime, later freezing when the temperature drops. Usually it is the seam welds that fail. Ponding over a soft area of fabric will severely affect the stability of a structure and introduce unpredicted loadings on cables and supports. And if allowance is not made for it, snow-loads can lead to the destruction of a membrane roof structure. Otto's West Germany Pavilion for Expo 67 survived until the winter of 1972–73 when maintenance and heating was discontinued, allowing snow to build up and the permissible loading of $100kp/m^2$ to be exceeded by a factor of two to three times. Eventually a mast broke and the roof around it collapsed. Even after it was damaged, the cable-net structure remained in a new state of equilibrium and slightly altered geometry. Modern tents are more robust than is sometimes realized.

GRAVITY'S LINE

Over the centuries, the heavy tile roofs of the farmhouses along Italy's Po Valley have sagged to the point where they now resemble the profiles of hanging chains. It is as though gravity has reclaimed the roofs to match the catenary (a self-defining line that illustrates how nature drifts towards the most logical shape), so that the roofs are more purely in tension. Suspension, or hanging, bridges exemplify the principle of pure tension. As one might expect, they arose in regions like the Himalayas and the Andes, which are disrupted by plunging mountain gorges and where there were suitable materials (such as bamboo and other fibrous plants) for cables. The application to architecture came much later, assisted by the development of iron chains and wire ropes. A direct descendant of the suspension bridge, the hanging roof is essentially a linear structure and is best suited to long, uninterrupted column-free spaces. Álvaro Siza's magnificent concrete hanging roof for the Portuguese Pavilion (p. 50) is an elegant example of the purity that such a simply expressed suspended roof can attain. Whilst such roofs frequently lack the genuine lightness and transparency of a suspended bridge, they make up for it with their clarity and expressive power.

Braga Stadium, Parque Norte, Braga (Portugal). Souto Moura Arquitectos.

ARCHITECT
Oscar Niemeyer, Rio de Janeiro (Brazil)

LOCATION
Hyde Park, London (UK)

PROJECT TEAM
Oscar Niemeyer, José Carlos Sussekind,
Jair Valera

INTEGRATED DESIGN
Arup, London (UK)

CONSTRUCTION
Sir Robert McAlpine Ltd, Hemel Hempstead (UK)

CLIENT
Luiz Inácio Lula da Silva, President of Brazil

COMPLETION
2003

Despite its limitations, Niemeyer's imitation tent for the Serpentine Gallery resonates powerfully with the surrounding parkland.

Each year the Serpentine Gallery, on the edge of the Serpentine in London's Hyde Park, commissions an artist to design a pavilion in its grounds to showcase contemporary architecture. In 2001, the pavilion was designed by Daniel Libeskind, and in 2002 Toyo Ito did the honours. In 2003 it was the turn of the ninety-six-year-old Brazilian architect Oscar Niemeyer, whose work is typically sensuous and sculptural. For this occasion, he chose a simple tent shape.

The stark white pavilion roof stood out against the green surroundings of Kensington Gardens. Niemeyer began with flowing freehand sketches, suggestions of the shape he was seeking to act as his theme. He had long ago rejected straight lines, believing that they isolated architecture from nature, and his pavilion was intended as an invitation to move freely between the two. The architect's first thought was to bury a space under an elevated platform, but Niemeyer eventually decided on a cantilevered platform lifted 1m above the ground and surmounted by a simple tent-like shape, falling to the platform tips. The floating floor echoed the plane of the green lawn, while the thick white sheet of roof rises up and ascends into the blue sky.

Suspended between two sets of uneven height masts, the roof was tied down at either end by straight planes. The roof and floor were painted white in contrast with the brilliant deep-red panels under the roof that hid the cross-bracing. An oval opening was cut at one end in the roof to expose the interior to the park. Along the front, the pavilion was reached by a stairway, and on the opposite side an angled ramp led down to the lawn. Inside, there was a scattering of bright yellow stools and seats.

Minimizing the number of walls kept it free of unwanted obstructions and liberated the pavilion space. The hanging tent roof acted on the space by causing it to spill sideways out over the grass. Of the finished work, Cecil Balmond, the chairman of Arup Europe, commented: 'We [had] imagined a park and a pavilion, nature and a piece of architecture, and Oscar Niemeyer intervening to place his magical mark on both.'

But Niemeyer failed to come to terms with the nature of his 'tensile' roof, which he framed in steel I-beam sections that supported the roof and hid the cross-bracing. The steel frame could not possibly be mistaken for a freely cascading tent cloth; it was much too thick and stiff and clearly falsified the very nature of a tent. What spectators were confronted with was a *symbolic* use of the tent. Niemeyer was creating a sculpture: the tent is only a starting point, the rest is art. In contrast, Ralph Twitchell and Paul Rudolph's wonderfully simple Healy Guest House (1948), also known as the 'Cocoon House', at Siesta Key, in Sarasota, Florida, is more believable though less impressive. Twitchell and Rudolph's roof is a membrane, its form looks natural. What Niemeyer succeeded in doing was using the tent shape to attach the pavilion to its landscape, and in the process imbuing it with a liberating sense of freedom.

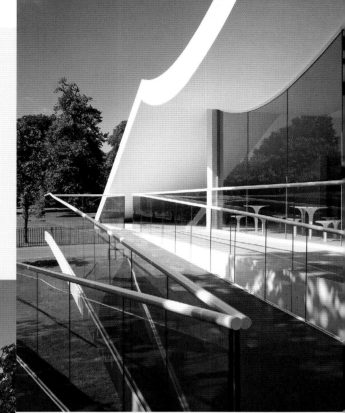

ARCHITECT
Álvaro Siza, Porto (Portugal)

LOCATION
Parque das Nações, Lisbon (Portugal)

ENGINEER
Arup, London (UK)

COMPLETION
1998

Álvaro Siza's concrete 'hanging' roof for the Portuguese Pavilion, an impressive technical achievement, covered an area of 3,500m².

The Portuguese Pavilion was a highlight of the Expo 98 programme. It consisted of the pavilion itself and a slightly raised, covered plaza of 65m x 50m, which supplied a dignified setting for both formal and informal events. The plaza, sited at the corner of the city's main boulevard and the axis from Oriente Station, and acting as a hinge between them, served as the entrance to the pavilion proper, where dignitaries were greeted and ceremonies officiated. Over the plaza, a 20cm-thick, curved concrete roof was supported symmetrically on either side by two porticoes.

From the city, the curved roof framed a view to the water. Projecting piers on either side resisted overturning moments from the roof. The roof was extremely thin for its 70m span (a ratio of 1:350). Its construction and proportions related directly to the space and were all carefully considered to maximize its architectural impact. From a height of 13m at its abutments, the roof fell to 10m at its lowest point, enough for the curve to register visually, yet not so great as to crush the space underneath it. The roof gave the strong impression that it was reduced to its absolute minimal essentials. Within this rigorous simplicity, it was highly refined and not without excitement and surprises. The concrete was suspended on a series of stainless-steel rods and terminated short of the sides, leaving a gap for the sun to shine through so that the roof appeared to float. The gap at each end was both aesthetic and integral to the construction. The heavy concrete was chosen to counter wind uplift, and the effect of its weight was neutralized by separating the roof from its abutment bearings. The cables alone crossed the two voids. At the lowest point in the roof, over the middle of the plaza, a thousand tons of concrete levitated in space. Siza's pavilion roof was one of the purest statements in recent architecture. It is rare to encounter a structure reduced to such a simple plane, hanging in defiance of gravity.

To avoid cracking, the concrete was de-bonded from the load-carrying system. An oiled sheath was provided for each cable to pass through, allowing the concrete to 'ride' the cable so that it (the cable) slipped through to neutralize the local effects of temperature and shrinkage over such a large span. Once the concrete had been poured onto the formwork and the cables fully stressed, the canopy lifted itself free of the shuttering and became a self-balancing system. The abutments were connected below ground to counter the roof pull and hold everything together. This completed the structural loop and closed the tension force in the air with a reverse line of thrust underground.

The two-storey main building to the north of the roof was slightly taller than the adjoining porticoes, and had a basement, separate public and VIP entrances, restaurants, an exhibition space, and a large, planted courtyard contrasting with the paved ceremonial plaza on the other side. Eduardo Souto de Moura, the architect of the Braga stadium (p. 54), designed the interior.

Rigorously calculated for structural integrity and safety, the massive concrete roof successfully projected the illusion of hovering perilously in space, defying gravity.

BRAGA STADIUM

ARCHITECT
Souto Moura Arquitectos, Porto (Portugal)

LOCATION
Monte Castro, Parque Norte, Braga (Portugal)

CONSULTANT
Arup, London (UK)

ENGINEER
AFA Associados, Porto and Lisbon (Portugal)

CLIENT
Câmara Municipal de Braga (Portugal)

COMPLETION
2003

Eduardo Souto de Moura's first idea for Braga's new football stadium was to create a thin, curved, continuous awning similar to Álvaro Siza's Portuguese Pavilion for Expo 98 (p. 50), but after a visit to Peru, where he was impressed by the extraordinary rope bridges of the Incas, he decided on the present slim stadium. Its roof awning, however, recalls the amphitheatre *vela* roof of Ancient Rome more than it does a swaying Inca bridge, and its strongest connection is with Siza's pavilion, whose structure it repeats. The pavilion's two gaps at the roof abutments have been omitted and replaced instead by a single, central opening over the playing field. Two stands replace the porticoes.

The city of Braga is noted for its religious festivals, and for being the ecclesiastical capital and seat of the country's archbishops. This temple to another kind of religion provides a focus for the new urban park planned around the slopes of Monte Castro and along the course of the River Cávado. The baroque theatricality of the stadium easily dominates its rugged mountain surroundings. Initially it was to be sited near the river, but was moved up the hillside due to the region's heavy rainfall. The 1,000,000m³ of stone that was removed to form the huge, rock-lined amphitheatre in which the stadium sits was later used in its new concrete super-structure.

Seating was removed from the goal-ends of the pitch and consolidated into two backward-canted stands, each seating 15,000 spectators in two overlapping tiers. The elimination of the cheaper seats behind the goals guaranteed optimum viewing for everyone. The stadium pitch is orientated northeast to southwest, with the northeast stand dug into the hillside and rising

against a backdrop of living rock that is approached from above via the main external plaza. This wall of rock is confronted by outward-leaning, heavy concrete piers and the undercroft of stairs, lifts and concourses, while on the opposite side, the second stand leans out at an angle on broad concrete blades like the ribs of a ship. Circular holes of varying diameters were punched into the concrete to reduce the overall mass, and staircases were inserted in between the structural blades. The two stands are shaded by lightweight roofs of ribbed metal panels slung between parallel series of steel tensile cables. The roof edges are stabilized laterally by lightweight V-section trusses that run along the leading edge. The trusses double as supports for the lighting gantry, thereby eliminating the necessity for intrusive floodlight towers.

Roof drainage is equally simple and direct. Freestanding, cantilevered concrete troughs collect the rainwater discharge at the roof edges and carry it down the hillside in open channels. This concrete rainwater structure is not only practical and easy to maintain, but is also an adjunct sculpture to the stadium, helping to lead the eye beyond the building into the landscape. The Braga stadium is a monumental hyperbole: its supports are much larger and heavier than seems really necessary, and its roof is so light as to seem almost incomplete. Like David and Goliath, the stadium's two parts struggle against each other, each determined to win.

The suspended cable awning of the concrete Braga stadium provides shelter for its two long stands.

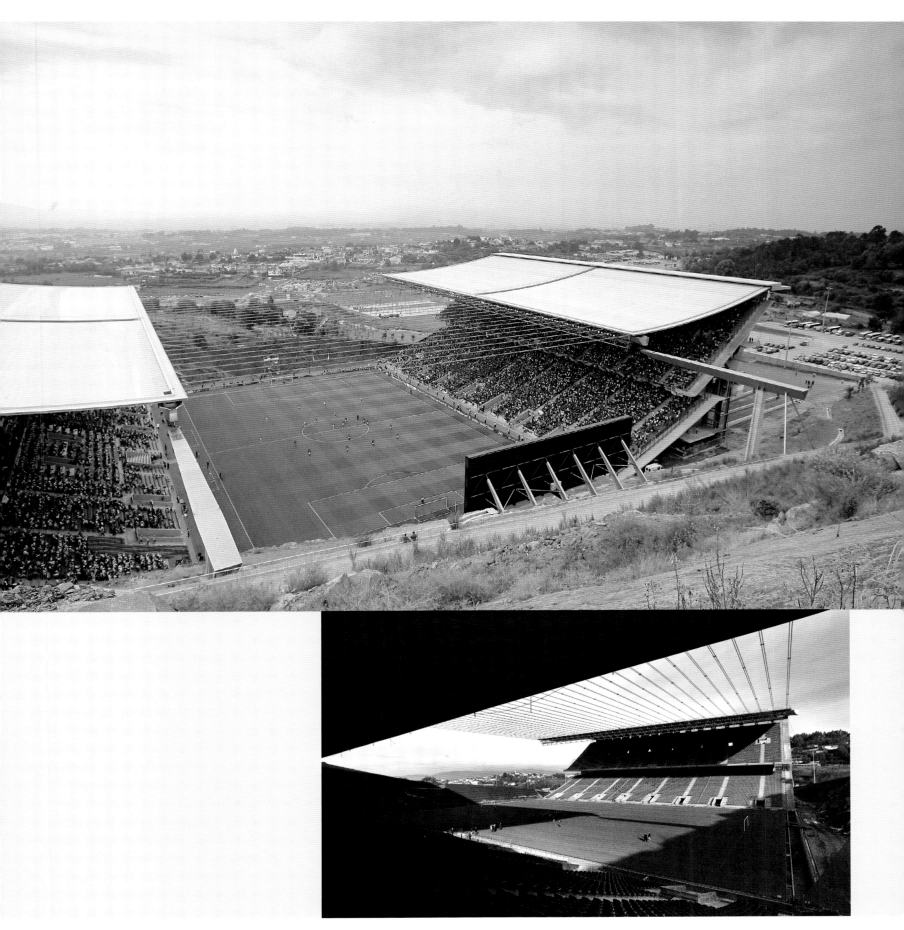

DAVID L. LAWRENCE CONVENTION CENTRE

ARCHITECT
Rafael Viñoly Architects,
New York, New York (USA)

LOCATION
Pittsburgh, Pennsylvania (USA)

ENGINEER
Dewhurst Macfarlane and Partners,
New York, New York (USA); Goldreich
Engineering, New York, New York (USA)

STRUCTURAL SYSTEM
ADF Group, Terrebonne, Quebec (Canada);
Birdair, Amherst, New York (USA)

MEMBRANE FABRICATOR
Birdair, Amherst, New York (USA)

CLIENT
Sports & Exhibition Authority,
Pittsburgh, Pennsylvania (USA)

COMPLETION
2003

**The outward-leaning shape of the
convention centre, hovering over the
Allegheny River, was designed to exist
in sympathetic harmony with the city's
three suspension bridges.**

Hanging structures seem especially suited to convention centres, which demand large, uninterrupted column-free exhibition spaces. The Allegheny River in Pittsburgh, spanned by three suspension bridges (known collectively as the 'Three Sisters'), seemed an ideal location for such a building. In this instance, the hanging roof relies on its weighty construction to resist uplift forces. Recalling the Castrop-Rauxel town centre building project in northern Germany of two decades earlier, the David L. Lawrence Convention Centre has a distinctive suspended roof supported by fifteen enormous cables.

On the north bank of the river, sets of outward-leaning columns, supporting the upper cantilevered floor decks, push against the cable load. The 294m-long roof is divided into fourteen bays, with spans measuring from 91m to 122m, suspended from steel masts along the south elevation. The back stay cables to the north terminate at exposed anchorages inside and on the concrete roof, where they can be seen by passers-by. In section, the building resembles a suspension bridge cut halfway at mid-span. Architect Rafael Viñoly called it 'half a bridge', in reference to Pittsburgh's suspension bridges.

The stainless-steel cladding of each roof-panel section is fixed to trusses between the pairs of strand cable. Glazed strips above eleven of the cables separate the metal roof deck to allow daylight into the main exhibition hall. The curve of the riverbank and the roof oppose each other: one tugs against the insistent pull of gravity, the other against the water's movement. A curtain of glass on the east and west sides isolates the roof from the building and allows it to float free. At night, with its underside acting as a giant light reflector, the exhibition hall is turned into an enormous glowing lantern.

Tents by their very nature are extremely economical, and this is especially true of the Pittsburgh convention centre. The upward slope of the roof towards the masts assists in naturally ventilating the exhibition hall by drawing cool air in from the river and venting warm air at the top. Fresh air is introduced during temperate months through louvres on both sides. When this is impossible, a system of paired fabric ducts with irregular perforations suspended from the roof allows diffuse air to enter the hall uniformly. Fabric ducts were cheaper to install than metal ductwork and are less prone to condensation with the energy-efficient, low-temperature HVAC (heating, ventilation and air-conditioning) system in use. A water-cooling system uses twin cascade fountains that line a nearby bypass as a heat exchange system.

A glazed bridge under the cable-and-truss supports of the roof on the second floor spans the main, column-free exhibition space. Fabric sunscreens were suspended behind the glass louvres under the cable roof to filter daylight. The David L. Lawrence Convention Centre exemplifies the convergence between lightweight tensile construction and energy-saving design; energy requirements have been reduced by a third for similar large buildings of the type. In 2003, the project earned a Gold LEED (Leadership in Energy and Environmental Design) rating from the US Green Building Council.

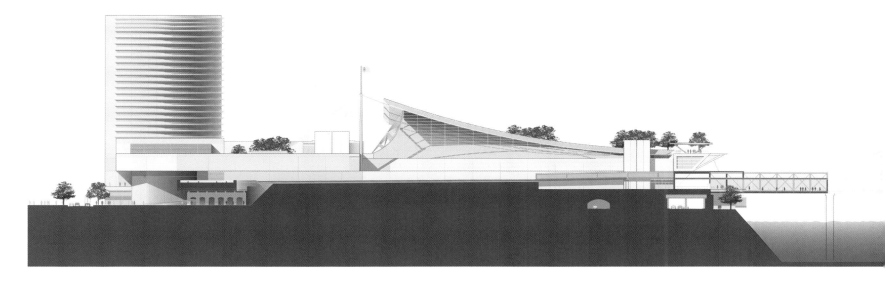

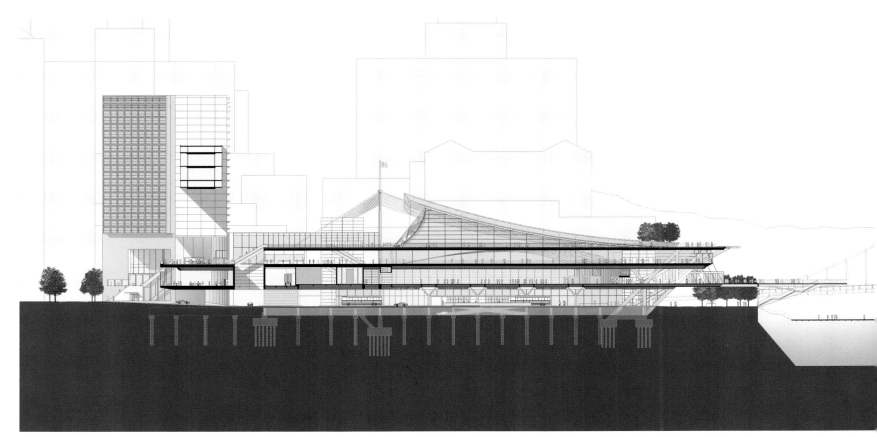

The stainless-steel clad hanging roof covers a vast area of 141, 750m². The centre's illuminated profile is an elegant focal point to the city's river vista.

SMALL PEAKS

Textile pavilions are naturally more limited in their span than are suspension bridges. This is due to the fact that stress is directly related to the radius of curvature in a fabric surface, with a radius of around 20m setting the upper limit. Because the thickness of the membrane is usually limited to around 1mm, this means that the maximum tensile strength is also limited. It is not simply a matter of making the material thicker to achieve a larger structure. Even strong modern fabrics such as PTFE-coated fibreglass (as used by Ackermann & Partner for their truck depot at Munich, see p. 70) have a nominal maximum size of roof element of around the 50m x 50m mark. By rethinking shapes and experimenting with novel combinations and arrangements of supports, a designer or architect can exercise great creativity in overcoming such limitations of span.

Longitude 131°, Ulurur-Kata Tjuta
National Park, Northern Territory
(Australia). Cox Richardson Architects.

ARCHITECT
Cox Richardson Architects, Sydney (Australia)

LOCATION
Ulurur-Kata Tjuta National Park, Northern Territory (Australia)

STRUCTURAL ENGINEERING
Robert Bird & Partners, Melbourne (Australia)

FABRICATOR
Taiyo Membrane Corporation, Queensland (Australia)

CLIENT
Bovis Lend Lease, New South Wales (Australia)

COMPLETION
2002

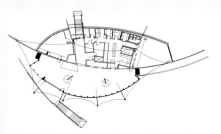

Springing to life after rain, the Australian Outback is a miraculous place, with the drab, rust-red emptiness suddenly replaced by a thick carpet of brilliant desert flowers. Not only is there no water, there is also an absence of shape: everywhere is flat. Such flatness demands curves, shapes that wrench free from the awful grip of the desert. With their delicacy and curvaceous shapes, tents strike a particular cadence in this harsh landscape.

In Aboriginal lore, Uluru (formerly known as Ayers Rock) is a sacred place inhabited by the snakes Liru and Kuniya. The huge monolith presents a formidable landmark, 9.6km in circumference with the furrowed red dome rising to 361m. The effects of weathering, particularly by the wind, are extraordinary: around its base are steep but short gullies, sweeping down from the summit and forming great buttresses. It is an impressive place, a spiritual sanctuary of the local people and an internationally, and instantly, recognized symbol of Australia.

Located within the Ulurur-Kata Tjuta National Park, Longitude 131° is a self-contained boutique hotel. Almost like modern Bedouins, tourists visit for a few days, staying in what is effectively a permanent camp. This causes environmental problems, such as the disposal of rubbish and waste and the increased stress on the desert ecology. The shelters are updated hybrid tents, using modern PVC superimposed on rigid, raised and prefabricated glass-and-steel enclosures. There are fifteen luxury 'guest-rooms', sited along a remote, crescent-shaped dune and serviced from a large tent containing the lounge and dining areas. At the rear, a masonry shell covered with a highly insulated metal roof deck houses the service facilities. Environmental concerns were addressed by raising each tent up on steel piles so that the sand is untouched, which also allows the rooms to be relocated if necessary without further disturbance. Compacted earth walkways are located on the low side of the dune to further protect the dune crest.

Like a seaman's oilskin sou'wester hat, the wide-brimmed, protective PVC membrane roofs are pulled down at the sides and turned up at the front. Each 80m² hotel room – a simple box with fully glazed, south-facing walls – opens onto a veranda, extending the interior and framing the spectacular views. Underneath the roof is a conventional prefabricated steel building. The attempt to combine the tent roof with such a basic structure is somewhat awkward. Moreover, the decision to make the rooms individual units rather than combining them in a larger tent fragments the form unduly, and results in a proliferation of small peaks that are too high and constrained for their small platforms.

The central 600m² dining/lounge pavilion on two steel poles is a better solution, but the generous communality of the pavilion is at odds with the jealous exclusivity of the individual units. The juncture of the tent roof with the building below is always difficult. Here, the hard steel frame cuts into the soft fabric form and feels uncomfortable, and assaults the curved, translucency of the roof. This disruption is avoided in the Bedouin black tent by making the walls and roof all the same fabric, which has the further advantage of allowing the tent to be reoriented when the wind changes direction. For all our advances in technology, we have yet to match the nomad's superior adaptation to desert life.

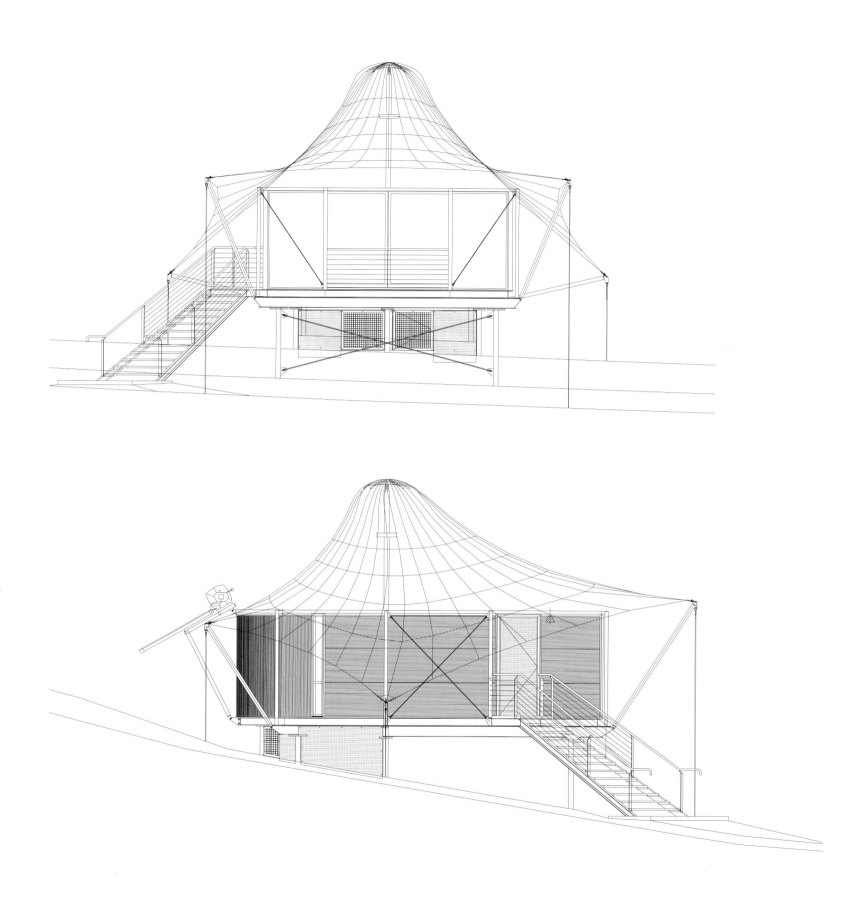

Each of the fifteen guesthouses is topped by a PVC-coated membrane roof. Also at the National Park is the 'Sails in the Desert' resort (right and p. 66), whose soaring fabric roofs complement the smaller guesthouses.

ARCHITECT
Ackermann & Partner, Munich (Germany)

LOCATION
Munich (Germany)

ENGINEER
Schlaich Bergermann, Stuttgart (Germany)

MEMBRANE FABRICATOR
Koch Hightex, Rimsting (Germany)

MEMBRANE CONSTRUCTION
Birdair Europe Stromeyer, Konstanz (Germany)

CABLE CONSTRUCTION
Pfeifer Seil- & Hebetechnik,
Memmingen (Germany)

CLIENT
Municipal Office for Waste
Management, Munich (Germany)

COMPLETION
2000

At the Munich truck depot, a PTFE-coated fibreglass membrane (1mm-thick) was used to cover an area of 8,400m².

The repeated structural motifs of La Mezquita, the great mosque at Cordoba, have an almost mesmerizing effect. How does the repetition of simple tiers of columns result in such great architecture? The answer depends, in part, on the sensual power of rhythm and geometry. The problem of reaching the mosque's high ceiling, perched on top of reused columns, was solved by placing one arch on top of the other. It was a simple and direct solution to a difficult construction challenge that is almost modern in its conception of transparent space reaching out to infinity. There is something profoundly moving about it, as if we see God in the distance. In a utilitarian truck depot at Munich, the seventy identical 10m x 12m bays, supported by steel columns, have a similarly disconcerting impact. Despite its mundaneness, the Munich depot is also a tour de force of architecture.

The basic bay of the garage is supported by eighty-eight steel columns on a standard 7m x 10m grid. The steel column substructure of the roof stands on a reinforced concrete deck, and the columns are protected from damaging impacts by concrete plinths. The membrane is negatively curved and restrained at the edge by cables, which reach inward and meet at the foot of a 4m flying strut that supports a ring high point above it. The ring is supported by four branches at the head of the flying strut. The suspended mast is made of tube sections, and a junction of cast steel at its foot can be adjusted in height. Four steel cables, 22mm in diameter, stretch from the column tops to the foot of the flying strut. The circular ring is strengthened by welding on an endless cable, 21mm in diameter, to it and to the membrane.

The standard membrane bays were fabricated from 12m-long, pre-cut strips welded together on site. Each of the membrane bays was prestressed by extending the central steel strut suspended on the underside to achieve the required prestress force. The principle is similar to the scissor-mast of the Algerian Berber tent, which stressed the tent cloth by drawing the feet of the two central masts closer together. The roof is drained through the hollow column using a vacuum system. The entire roof was designed as a structurally continuous area, with thin cables on top of the skin framing the uniform bays. None of the members of this lightweight construction is subject to bending. The space under the canopy is modulated by the columns, the up-curved edge cables framing each bay, and the dark, radial membrane seams rising to peaks above the cable-supported struts at each centre. Like that of La Mezquita, the construction of the Munich truck depot is very simple and quite spellbinding.

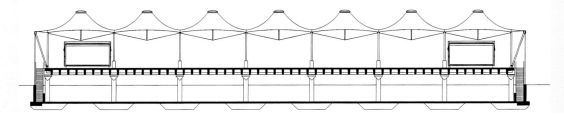

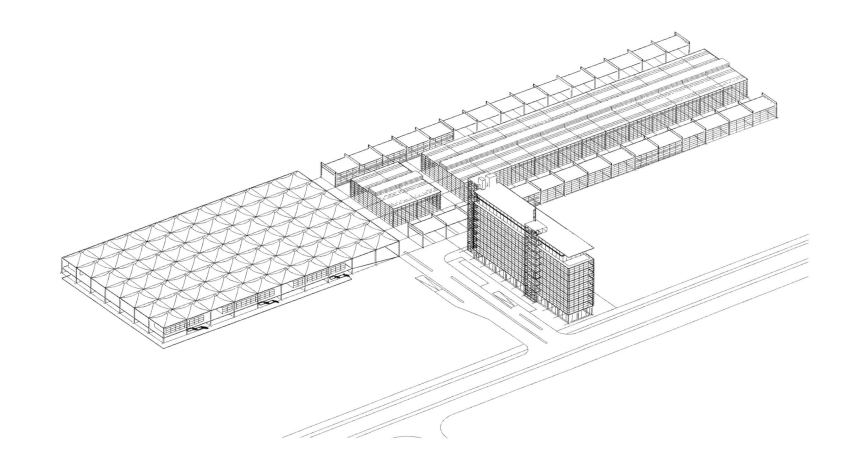

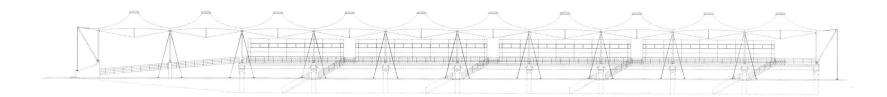

The membrane roof, punctuated by dark, radial seams and supported by uniformly spaced steel columns, provides shelter for the brightly coloured trucks below.

The repetition of snowy fabric
peaks is a striking architectural
statement in simplicity.

ARCHITECT
Hopkins Architects, London (UK)

LOCATION
Buckingham Palace, Green Park, London (UK)

ENGINEER
Arup, London (UK)

CANOPY FABRICATOR
Landrell Fabric Engineering, Chepstow (UK)

COMPLETION
1995

The Buckingham Palace ticket office, in use from 1995 to 2000 and now replaced by a new facility near the Queen's Gallery, was only used for two months, August and September, during each year of its life. It was gently curved, taking its geometry from the radius of the nearby monument to Queen Victoria. The fabric roof, whether inspired directly by tents or by yacht masts and rigging, reinforced the structure's temporary character.

The building was a modest construction consisting of a smooth wooden cabin, shaped like a caravan, and a membrane roof fashioned from Modacrylic, a lightweight, translucent fabric resembling canvas, suspended from a pair of elliptical glulam (glue-laminated timber) masts at each end. A main keel beam above the teller windows was bolted to the columns by stainless-steel plates spliced into the glulam masts. At 3m centres, a series of struts was connected on both sides to the keel. A series of transverse cables travelled from the top of the masts and formed a connecting catenary cable to more stainless-steel plates at the ends of the perpendicular struts, and on down to ground anchorages. The masts were stabilized longitudinally at both ends by concrete anchor blocks, and linked above the ticket cabin by an axial catenary cable. This cable picked up the 'coat hangers' from which the fabric roof was suspended, thus giving the membrane its humped profile. The roof, though much smaller, recalled other fabric roofs by Michael Hopkins, notably those at the Summer Pavilions at Goodwood racecourse in West Sussex (p. 80) and the Inland Revenue building in Nottingham. The Buckingham Palace ticket office was effectively a miniature version of these other roofs.

The ticket cabin was a prefabricated construction in two parts, which were brought separately to the site and bolted together. It rode on small wheels so that it could be towed away at the end of the season. Externally, 67mm x 18mm-thick boards of Western Red Cedar were fastened to 25mm birch-faced plywood ribs at 750mm centres, which were bolted to a steel chassis. The cedar was finished inside and out with a yacht varnish to intensify the rich colour. The corners were rounded to give a totally smooth and flush finish. In keeping with its tent construction, fresh air was taken from under the ticket cabin and stale air was exhausted naturally though a series of rooflights that kept the interior bright. Electrical conduits were hidden in cable trays in the chassis. Like a tent, the ticket office was designed to be demountable, storable and durable. At the time it was commissioned, it was anticipated that the structure would be used for five years.

An axial catenary cable catches the Modacrylic membrane at intervals, and gives the roof its peaked appearance.

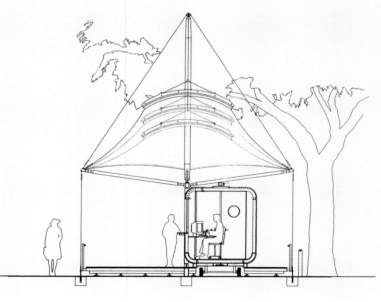

The ticket office, huddled at the edge of Green Park between the palace and the Queen Victoria memorial, was a popular tourist destination.

ARCHITECT
Hopkins Architects, London (UK)

LOCATION
Goodwood, West Sussex (UK)

ENGINEER
Arup, London (UK)

COMPLETION
2001

Racetracks are outdoor theatre, where the game of luck is played out in front of the stands. It is the architect's responsibility to properly choreograph this scene of victory. Because of their connection with the nobility, tents and marquees have long been associated with the track, along with other English grass sports, which were traditionally viewed from tents. A day at the races, above all, is a social occasion and a spectacle to which tents lend an air of gaiety, colour and glamour.

Goodwood, located within the ancestral estate of the Duke of Richmond, is one of England's most prestigious racetracks. Its principal activities are now reorganized by three hovering PVC 'hats' suspended from masts, whose minimal structure gives the trackside a wonderful summery feel. There are four Parade Ring structures, plus a canopy over the weighing-in area. Goodwood previously had a haphazard back-of-grandstand, and the movement of people from the March Stand (built by Howard Cobb in 1980) to the ring was obstructed by the jockeys' weighing-in building. The new layout creates an entrance and drop-off point, ticket office and meeting room, improving the working of the course. The three tent pavilions directly overlook the winner enclosures, with the new weighing-in facility underneath the central pavilion. The symmetrical grouping and visibility of the pavilions add greatly to the sense of occasion on race day. From the terrace, the pageant of people and horses can be watched and enjoyed to the full.

The pavilions are similar to Michael Hopkins' earlier Mound Stand at Lord's Cricket Ground (1987), in London. Two masts at each end support a central catenary cable, from which secondary hanger cables descend to the membrane canopy. The catenary support cable is anchored to the ground by end stay cables. Everything is planned around this structure, with a central bar, or servery, surrounded by tables and balconies overlooking the grassed paddock. The middle pavilion is open and has tall tables for standing clients, from which can be seen breathtaking views of the enclosure and beyond to the beautiful countryside and Chichester cathedral, and in the far distance, the North Sea.

Tents have a natural advantage over architecture when it comes to engaging the landscape. Their upswept shape, combined with an ethereal cloud-like suspended quality, reinforces the impression of lightness. The three multi-peaked pavilions at Goodwood suggest a medieval tournament: there is the anticipation of exciting events to come, the splash of fashion, and the crush of the crowd concentrated under lucent pavilions. Everything begins to float like a dream under the unbearable lightness of the tents.

PVC-coated polyester membrane forms the roof for the three pavilions, each supported by two end masts.

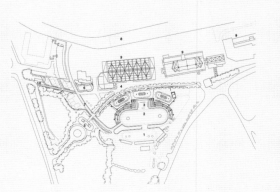

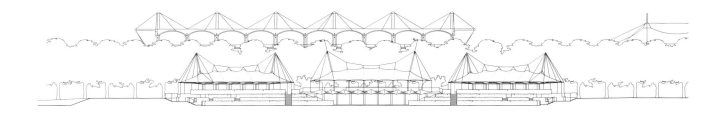

The use of fabric roofs at sporting events enhances visibility for the spectators, and injects a sense of occasion and glamour to the proceedings.

LARGE WAVES

A scale limit was soon reached in traditional tensile building beyond which it was difficult to proceed without a stronger support structure, but a jump in technology in the 1960s led to a new type of super-tent with superior spanning capabilities. At about the same time, coated fibreglass fabrics began to be produced which made tents more durable and led to more highly engineered large fabric structures. With these advances, membranes could compete with conventional buildings in an expanded range of applications. In 1972 a transparent roof was erected over the Olympic stadium to minimize dark shadows on the ground, a feat that could not have been achieved before and was only possible with a minimal prestressed, cable-net roof. But greater size brings with it greater structural complexity, and enlarged constructions become weaker due to the increasing burden of self-weight. Tensile structures, however, are lightweight to begin with, and gravity plays a less important role in span-limitation. Consequently, multi-layered nets with membrane liners can be made very large with respect to the tensile strength of the cables. Super-tents mark a turning point in new tent architecture, as fabric structures become environments in their own right that participate in the landscape.

Dynamic Earth Centre, Edinburgh (UK).
Hopkins Architects.

CHEMICAL RESEARCH CENTRE

ARCHITECT
Samyn & Partners, Brussels (Belgium)

LOCATION
Venafro (Italy)

STRUCTURAL ENGINEER
Setesco, Brussels (Belgium)

CLIENT
M&G Ricerche, Venafro (Italy)

COMPLETION
1991

Supported on six lattice arches, the PVC-coated polyester membrane covers an area of 2,700m², with a footprint of 85m (length) x 32m (width) x 15m (height).

Fabric structures suit laboratories because they are flexible and provide natural daylighting. Samyn & Partners' research centre in the Volturno valley, east of Rome, is roughly similar to Michael Hopkins' earlier Schlumberger Research Laboratories in Cambridge, but it is unlike that project structurally. Whereas the fabric roof of the latter is suspended from four kingposts, like a circus big top, that of the former is supported by lattice arches.

The client required a research centre with controlled environmental laboratories and offices, and the possibility of erecting test rigs later. Among several options were separating the functions into different buildings, or (the architect's favoured approach) placing them side-by-side in a single volume under a large tent structure that sheltered the rigs in relatively stable climatic conditions. Although the different functions are housed in the same space, they are segregated to permit the environmental control to be adjusted to the more sedentary activities on the perimeter.

In all tensile structures, the membrane must be supported by masts, by some other nearby structure, or by arches, as is the case here, where six triangulated, compression-loaded arches of tubular steel rise from an oval plan and transmit the loads to the footings. The size of the arches increases from the two ends to achieve a maximum height of 15m in the middle, and inclines outward away from the central, highest arch to receive five stabilizing cables that run lengthwise. These cables are contained within the PVC-coated polyester fabric roof and are secured to the lattice arches by means of downward-pointing tubular steel pyramids.

Between the arches, the fabric assumes a gently curved, anticlastic saddle shape that terminates above the ground floor to leave room for windows around the perimeter. These have generous views to the outside to counteract any feeling of being smothered by the enclosing translucent fabric (the uniform quality of daylight under fabric structures can prove monotonous, and even stifling, in its lack of contrast). At this research laboratory, the strips below the projecting lattice arches are covered by semi-transparent PVC, which lets broad bands of sunlight penetrate the interior to give welcome relief from the uniformity of the light, as well as affording glimpses of the sky.

The internal structures are conventional, in-situ concrete blocks with concrete infill. Tapered steel brackets support elegant steel balconies that give access to a two-storey building. The walkways are reached by steel stairs, which are exposed as they rise up inside the tent volume. Access to the centre is from opposite sides of the tent: on the south for people, and on the north for arriving goods.

The chemical research centre is surrounded by water to prevent people from getting too close to the fabric cover. The water also attaches the large tent to its immediate surroundings in a grove of olive trees, which serves as a reminder of the traditional economy in the area. The olives between the laboratory and the clearly visible outline of the nearby mountains form a transition zone. With its lights on at night, the half-oval of the laboratory is completed by its inverted reflection, turning it into a large, illuminated shape in the surrounding darkness.

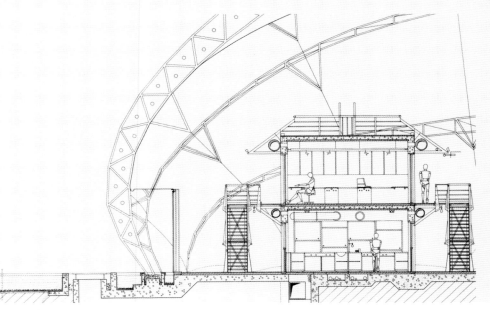

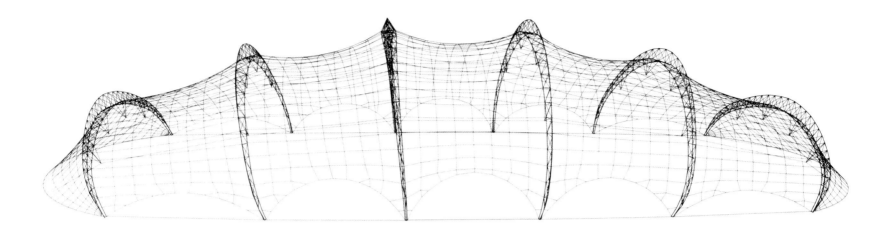

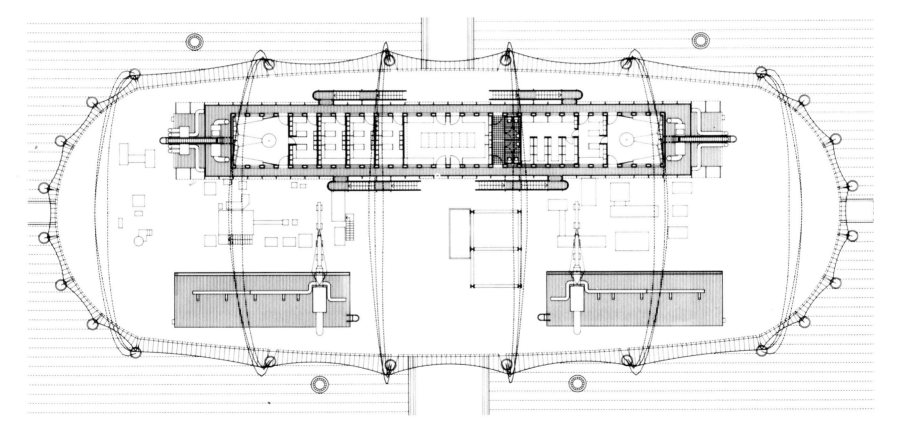

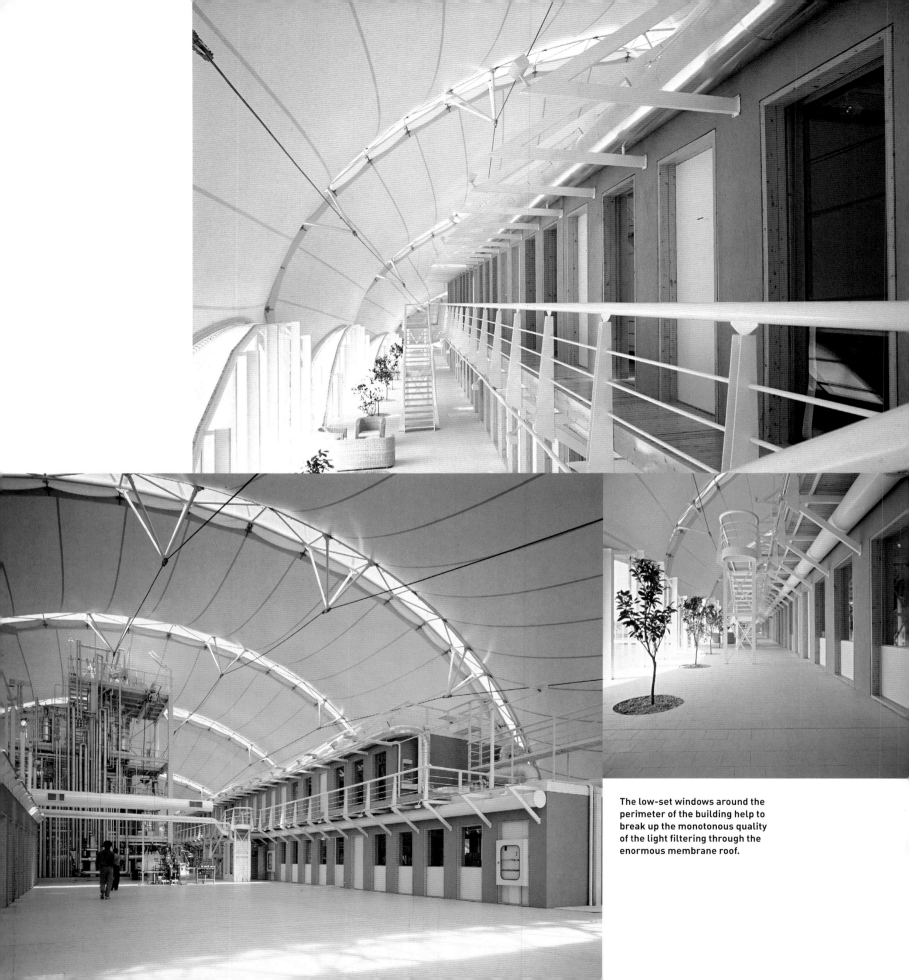

The low-set windows around the perimeter of the building help to break up the monotonous quality of the light filtering through the enormous membrane roof.

At night, the illumination from within and the reflection below turn the research centre into a beautiful glowing form, sitting gently within the landscape.

ARCHITECT
Fentress Bradburn Architects, Denver, Colorado

LOCATION
Denver, Colorado

ASSOCIATE ARCHITECTS
Bertram A. Bruton & Associates, Denver, Colorado; Harold Massop Associates, Denver, Colorado; Pouw & Associates, Denver, Colorado

STRUCTURAL ENGINEER
Severud Associates, New York, with Horst Berger, White Plains, New York

FABRIC
Birdair, Amherst, New York

CLIENT
City and County of Denver

COMPLETION
1995

One of the very earliest applications of membrane architecture was for airport terminals. Frei Otto's structures for Expo 67 and the 1972 Munich Olympics pointed to the super-tent's potential, but it was Skidmore, Owings & Merrill's Haj Terminal in 1980 that fully demonstrated it by realizing the largest membrane roof construction in the world at the time. At Denver International Airport, the aim of the project from the outset was to create a memorable piece of civic architecture – a goal that has certainly been achieved in the new terminal's white fabric peaks, which complement the picturesque Rocky Mountains much as the peaks and valleys of Otto's roofs for the Munich Olympics echoed the nearby Bavarian Alps.

In his early sketches, architect Curtis Fentress introduced the idea of a roof that would evoke the sparkling, snow-clad mountains and sought to capture the adventure of flight by enlarging the space in the new terminal. In recognition of the city's Western heritage, the outdoors were brought inside and the interior and exterior spaces fused (Eero Saarinen achieved much the same effect at Dulles International Airport in 1962).

The conceptual models for the project showed a succession of wave membranes covering the central space. Its fabric roof is supported off two rows of seventeen masts, spaced 20m apart, and held in place by two sets of primary cables. The arrangement was refined in later roof/mast-structure assembly studies. The 305m x 50m roof is sectioned into thirds to facilitate a greater height over the cross-bridge connections. Daylight is admitted through the roof, and additional skylights at each peak and a triangular-shaped clerestory around the

periphery increase the flood of natural light into the Great Hall, virtually eliminating the need for artificial lighting. Through the masthead skylights, travellers can catch glimpses of the sky and see what the weather conditions are like outside.

The fabric is tensioned by cables, including ridge cables that take the downward load of snow and self-weight of the roof, and valley cables that resist upward forces from the wind. A third set of cables, arranged about 12m apart and at right angles, is encased in fabric sleeves in the outer membrane and take the anticipated stresses when a panel of fabric is replaced. The roof comprises two layers of woven fibreglass fabric coated with Teflon: an outer layer is the primary tensile structure, and an inner layer serves as an acoustic barrier and screen hiding the seams. An air space between the two layers of 40cm to 160cm provides added thermal insulation.

The junction of fabric roof with rigid walls is a recurring problem in tensile architecture. The vertical movement of the fabric is dealt with here by leaving a gap between the roof edge and the upper edge of the cantilevered glass wall, and closing it with pneumatic tubes, 60cm in diameter and known as 'sausages', which expand and contract as the fabric moves. This detail is repeated at the north and south ends of the Great Hall.

The membrane roof of the Denver terminal, in marked contrast to the predictable architecture of the nearby support buildings, creates a sense of arrival and intimates something of the adventurous spirit for which the Wild West is renowned. The cowboys have long since departed, but their spirit lives on in the flying white peaks of Denver International Airport.

Denver's new airport terminal, serving 72 million passengers a year, is covered by a two-layer, Teflon-coated fibreglass membrane roof, reinforced with cables.

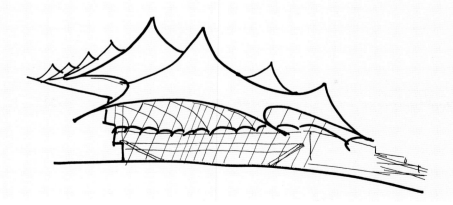

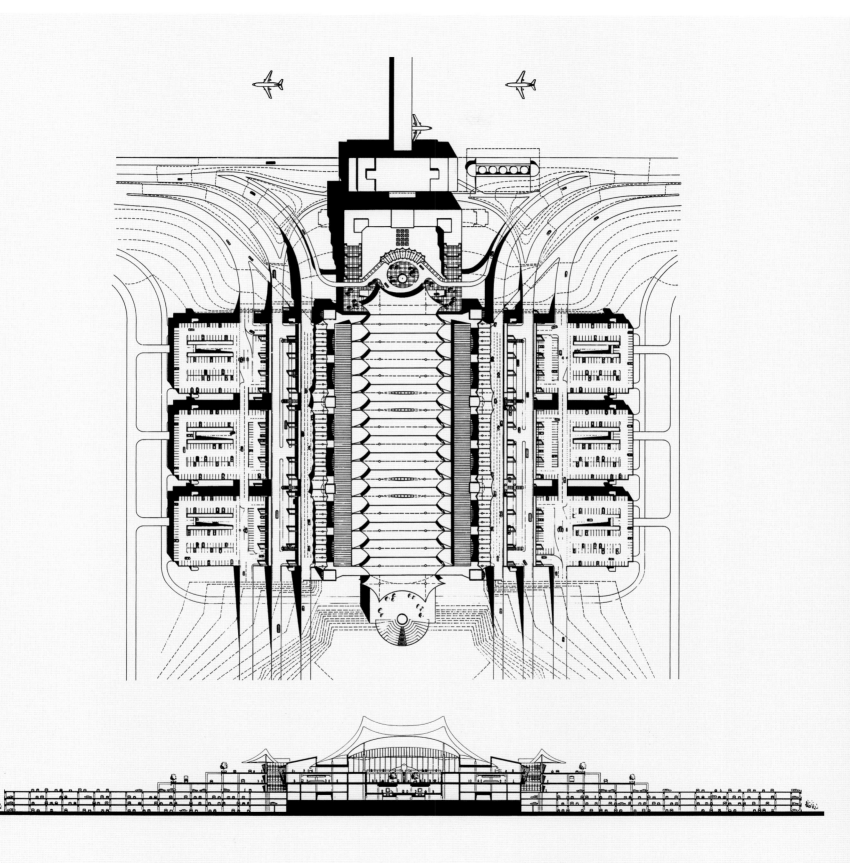

The succession of tented peaks forming the new terminal's roof provide both maximum light inside and a striking counterpoint to the rugged landscape.

ARCHITECT
Roy Mänttäri, Helsinki (Finland)

LOCATION
Hamina (Finland)

CLIENT
National Board of Antiquities and
Historical Monuments, Helsinki (Finland)

COMPLETION
1998

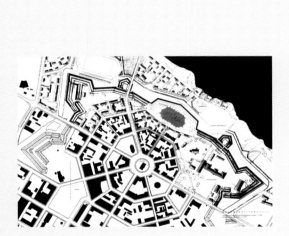

Spanning the central bastion of
Hamina's coastal defences, the PVC-
coated polyester membrane roof
covers an area of 5,800².

To the east of Helsinki, the town of Hamina faces the Gulf of Finland. Its rigid radial/octagonal plan is surrounded by a Vauban-style encircling fortification (referring to the 17th-century military engineer Sébastien le Prestre de Vauban) of seven bastions that were built by the Russians in the 19th century, and restored by prisoners from the Hamina penal colony in 1998. A central bastion with fifty-eight arched brick storehouse casements is the largest and most recent of the six surviving bastions. Upkeep of the works is guaranteed by an agreement between the town and the National Board of Antiquities and Historical Monuments.

A shelter of some kind was required inside the bastion to protect public events, but it was important that it did not compete with the brick fortification, was economical, airy in appearance and could be easily removed. The dimensions for the roof needed to be large enough to protect the 30m x 60m parade ground and a seated audience of 4,000. Since the bastion is bisected by a radial street through the inner wall from the town centre, architect Roy Mänttäri consequently fitted his membrane structure, consisting of four waves alternating with valleys, within the bastion so that it straddled the street axis symmetrically at right angles to the long axis.

The structure is simple: each ridge is supported by ropes on pairs of unequal tapered, triangle-section steel masts that rise in a V-formation from a common foundation. Alternating ridge and valley cables deform the fabric, and valley ropes in between each ridge pull the membrane down against uplift forces. The membrane is lifted to permit the anchor cables to pass above the brick casements to anchorages high on the fortification wall,

and the wave-shaped, non-inflammable PVC-coated polyester fabric (less than 1mm thick) is stabilized by cable tension. Its fabric strips, accentuated by shadow, run lengthwise to emphasize the alternating ridge-and-valley canopy profile. Twisted steel cables, capable of withstanding 50 tons, anchor the roof to the base rock. The flying canopy is kept well clear of the beautiful old casement walls, and, like the town layout, it too is symmetrical. Its arresting peaked silhouette has been kept low and unobtrusive to avoid any suggestion of competition with the town hall and church spires that dominate Hamina's skyline.

The contrast between the lightweight translucent canopy and the heavy brick fortification is full of drama. It is somewhat reminiscent of the deliberate juxtaposition in Thomas Telford's suspension bridge over the Menai Straits of tapered Gothic stone pylons against the delicate weightlessness of the bridge's iron chains and hangers (see p. 23). In the bright summer sunshine, the glowing Hamina canopy lightly floats in defiance of gravity, dancing playfully while the bastion marches to a sombre military beat. The membrane shape truthfully explains the forces on it, as they flow down masts to anchorages and foundation supports. Structural narrative and fabric shape come together in visual complicity.

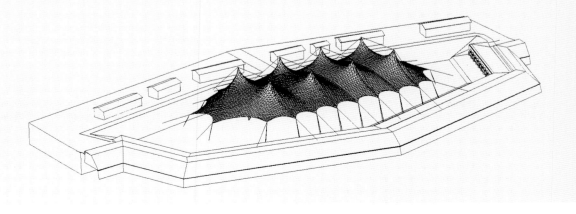

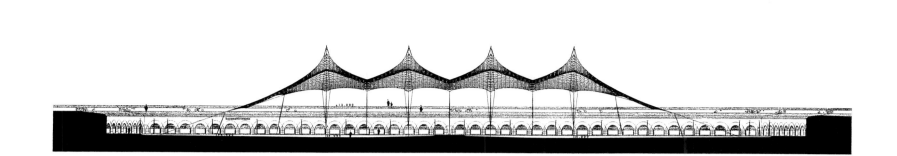

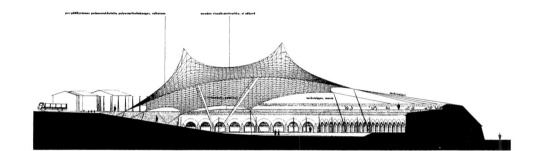

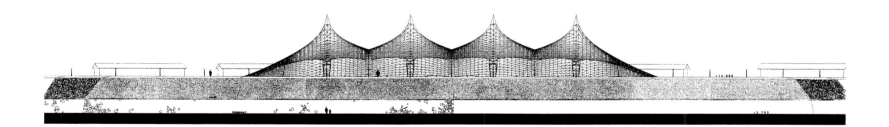

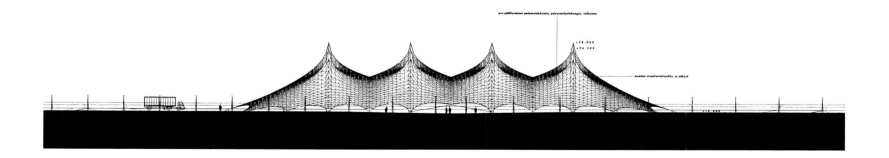

Every year the Hamina Tattoo, a military music event, is held under the central bastion's soaring canopy. The venue also provides ample space for theatre performances, concerts, exhibitions and sporting events.

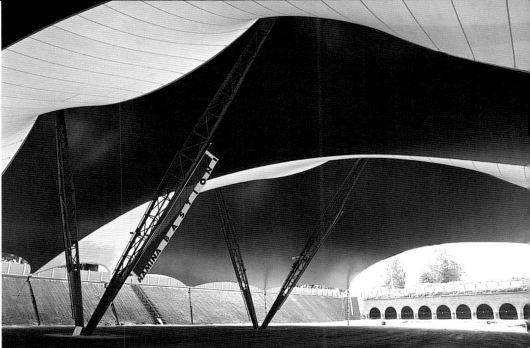

ARCHITECT
Samyn & Partners, Brussels (Belgium)

LOCATION
Brussels (Belgium)

COMPLETION
1999

Membrane-covered buildings are a very practical and economic way to protect railway platforms. With their lightness of weight and association with portability, they are also suggestive of travel, but only rarely is this connection honoured. The light fabric roofs covering the central platform of this train station, however, are a welcome exception.

Reached by two tunnels leading to the hospital and street, access to the platform is dramatic. Travellers emerge from the depths of the railway tunnels into a world flooded with filtered daylight, covered by a succession of eleven identical saddle-shaped roofs. The roofs possess an expansive airiness that is quite unexpected and liberating after the confinement and darkness of the tunnels. Each of the eleven roofs is supported by inverted-V steel structures that resemble high-tension electric power-line pylons, with the important difference that these towers are covered and concealed from the outside. From these 'pylons', curved, coat hanger-shaped frames cantilever out over the two railway tracks on either side of the central platform.

The project posed the question of what shape would make the best extensive linear shelter. The answer, not surprisingly, was an updated, extended version of the traditional Bedouin black tent. In this instance, the edges of the saddle-shaped membrane are tensioned by edge cables that are stretched between the pylon arms. The translucent fabric hangs in soft, convex folds between the frames, with the panel joins running lengthwise, their dark seams emphasizing the roof's curved surface. Each frame is connected to the other and anchored to the ground by cables. But while the roof solved the problem of shelter, it failed to protect the interior from wind and rain, and side walls, made of cone-shaped curtains of stainless-steel fabric, were duly added. The steel fabric is translucent and allows passengers waiting on the platform to see the world outside.

At this railway station in Brussels, a PVC-coated polyester membrane roof is used in conjunction with woven stainless-steel fabric walls.

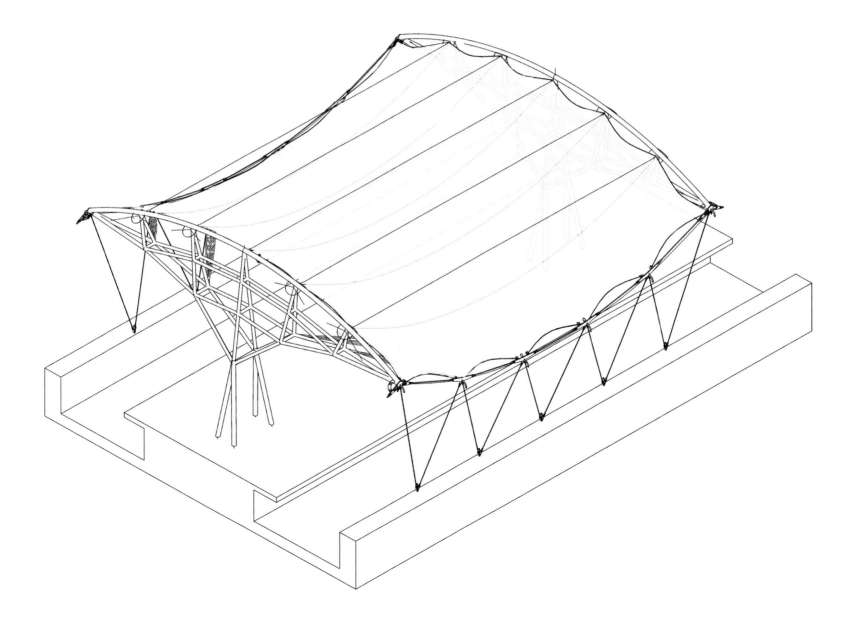

LARGE WAVES / BRUSSELS RAILWAY STATION

The shape of the structure is an updated version of the traditional Bedouin black tent. Here, the edges of the membrane are tensioned by edge cables stretched between inverted-V steel 'pylons'.

The eleven identical saddle-shaped roofs over the railway station's central platform are a striking addition to the Brussels skyline.

ARCHITECT
Ingenhoven Overdiek Architekten,
Düsseldorf (Germany)

LOCATION
Stuttgart (Germany)

ENGINEER
Leonhardt, Andrä & Partner, Stuttgart
(Germany), with Happold Ingenieurbüro,
Berlin (Germany)

CONSULTANT
Frei Otto, Leonburg (Germany)

CLIENT
Deutsche Bahn, Berlin, represented
by DB Projekte Süd, Stuttgart (Germany)

PROJECTED COMPLETION
2013

**The architects' scheme for the Stuttgart
main railway station has been designed
as an 'integrated ecological concept',
and has won many awards to back its
eco aspirations.**

This competition-winning scheme for the new main station at Stuttgart applies an innovation of Frei Otto's from the 1960s: a cable-loop that spreads load more evenly and avoids destructive concentrations of stress at the mastheads. The Stuttgart proposal, which is to be located next to the existing 1922 railway station by Paul Bonatz, incorporates cable-loop 'light eyes' to create an undulating terrain over the railway platforms underneath. It is a hardened and more disciplined version of Otto's roofscape for Expo 67, where transparent eye-holes allowed daylight to flood into the interior and simultaneously dramatize the meeting of mast connection with cable roof. This beautiful arrangement is repeated here in a very sculptural manner, making the most of the roof's opening to relieve the customary claustrophobic effect of such large subterranean spaces.

The project is in the tradition of the pioneer generations of railway stations in the 19th century, but introduces new engineering ideas. As part of an ambitious plan by Deutsche Bahn to add a new high-speed line to a European-wide network by providing an underground tunnel at right angles to the existing tracks, the station will be linked to and will rejuvenate the old Bonatz terminus, and will free up the surrounding urban quarter. The further addition of a square and parks, it is hoped, will also promote the area as a centre of social activity.

The architects' scheme will stretch the park adjoining the existing station over the top of the railway racks, and translate the new era of rail transportation into a contemporary form, in much the same way that Nicholas Grimshaw's International Terminal at London's Waterloo (now superseded by St Pancras)

did. But the Stuttgart proposal is closer to Grimshaw's 2006 Southern Cross Station (see p. 32) in Melbourne, with its multi-domed roof supported 23m off the platforms on giant steel trees. The funnel cable anchorages are now hollow mushroom columns, which expand vertically to present cable-loop shapes that pierce the garden roof and allow sunlight to penetrate inside. The efficient compression shell structure is estimated to reduce the amount of material required for its construction to 1/100.

Experiments with soap-film models anchored by cable-loops were used at the beginning to determine the eventual form of the roof, followed by an investigation with suspended chains in a hexagonal net and stiffened fabric. All this helped to solidify the concept and establish what might result from dragging the surface underground through holes by simulating the opening up of the ceiling to the sky and city above the station. The result at ground level is a flat plane broken by transparent bubbles that swell into graceful mounds with large eyes through which pedestrians can watch the trains and support under-structure below ground.

The new station has been approached as a 'zero energy' solution, and will operate without energy being required to heat or cool or mechanically ventilate the platform area. This demanded close cooperation between the architects and engineers. The station's shell roof will draw air upwards through the skylight eyes, and allow sunlight to penetrate and warm the tracks in winter. The station will not only be economical to operate, but its novel form will also advance the high-speed concept of rail travel in the 21st century that builds on the earlier 19th-century tradition.

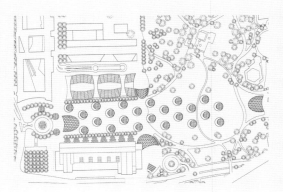
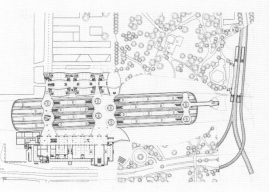

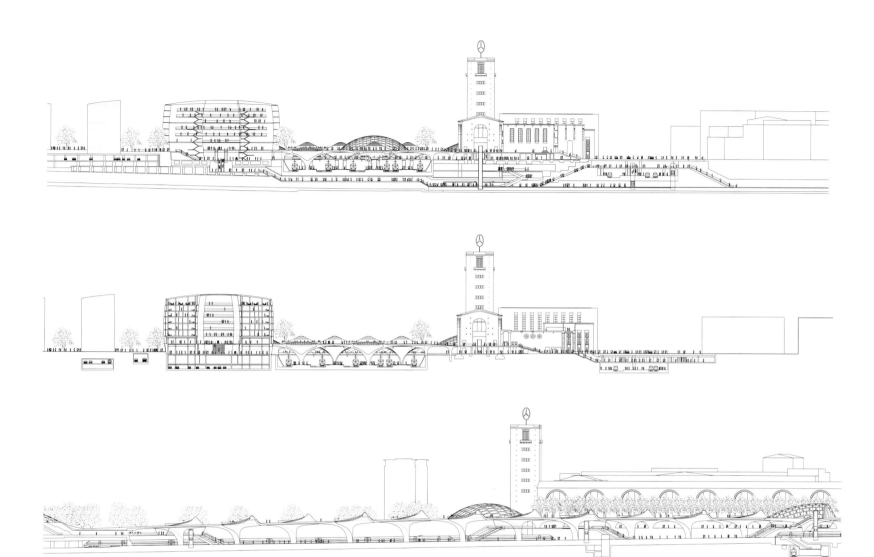

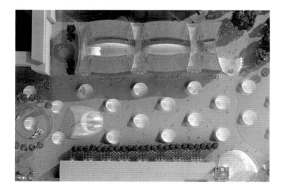

LARGE WAVES / STUTTGART MAIN STATION

The futuristic-looking 'light eyes' pulled down from the roof into the station's interior are actually an adaptation of Frei Otto's experiments with cable-loops in the 1960s.

ARCHITECT
Richard Rogers Partnership, London (UK)

LOCATION
Greenwich, London (UK)

STRUCTURAL AND SERVICES ENGINEER
Büro Happold, London (UK)

MEMBRANE ENGINEERING
Birdair Europe Stromeyer, Konstanz (Germany)

CLIENT
Millennium Commission, London (UK)

COMPLETION
2000

Half a century separates Ralph Tubbs' 'Dome of Discovery' for the 1951 Festival of Britain from the Millennium Dome, which, situated beside the River Thames on the Greenwich peninsula, is a deceptive anti-monument of arresting simplicity. It is easy to miss its link to the familiar circus big top. At 80,000m², it is the largest fabric structure in the world. The scene from the film *The World is Not Enough*, in which James Bond is snagged by the external guy cables that stabilize the dome, indicates the truly gigantic scale of the building, which dominates its flat peninsular landscape. Nelson's Column could easily stand within its cavernous interior.

Twelve bright yellow, 100m-high steel lattice masts – mounted on 10m-high plinths, in a 200m ring – support the dome. The masts support an intricate network of steel cables. A 30m-diameter steel cable tension rooflight holds the fabric at the centre; around the perimeter, a compression beam resists the inward pull and vertically anchors the dome to the ground. The central opening has mechanically opening vents that allow the structure to be ventilated naturally. The hemispherical dome is clad with Teflon-coated fibreglass fabric in seventy-two tensioned steel stringer cables, 32mm in diameter, arranged radially in pairs. The cable pairs run in a star pattern to the central compression cable ring. The ring on top of the dome consists of twelve 48mm cables. Should one fail, the safety of the dome is unaffected. The radial cables are held in position by upper hanger and lower tie-down cables at a radial spacing of 25–30m from masts anchored to the ground by guy cables. The detailing of the connection of the thirty-two cables that come together at the mastheads was extremely demanding.

The roof load is distributed between the stressed roof skin through distortion and the radial tensioned cables prestressed with a force of 400kN, about 66 per cent of the maximum permissible tension to achieve adequate rigidity. Panels of medium-weight PTFE-coated fibreglass fabric are stretched between the radial cables. The precise shape of the fabric panels was carefully designed to ensure the surface acquired the desired form and achieved the required tension. More than 20,000 aluminium screw clamps were used to attach the roof skin to the steel cables. A double-layer construction was adopted to avoid condensation on the underside of the fabric. An advantage of the porous inner membrane is its superior acoustic absorption, but on account of this it is more susceptible to soiling.

The smooth fabric is opaque during the day, but at night glows eerily like a giant jellyfish. The mechanical and service equipment is housed in pods encased in slatted cylindrical cages distributed around the perimeter, keeping it out of sight and thereby solving what is a common problem in minimal surface structures. The enormous size of the Millennium Dome, combined with its structural economy, recalls the earlier Utopian architectural suggestions by such pioneers as Buckminster Fuller and Frei Otto, who envisaged megastructures capable of housing entire human communities within their own separate, controlled microclimates.

The world's largest membrane structure incorporates a two-layer PTFE-coated fibreglass fabric panel membrane.

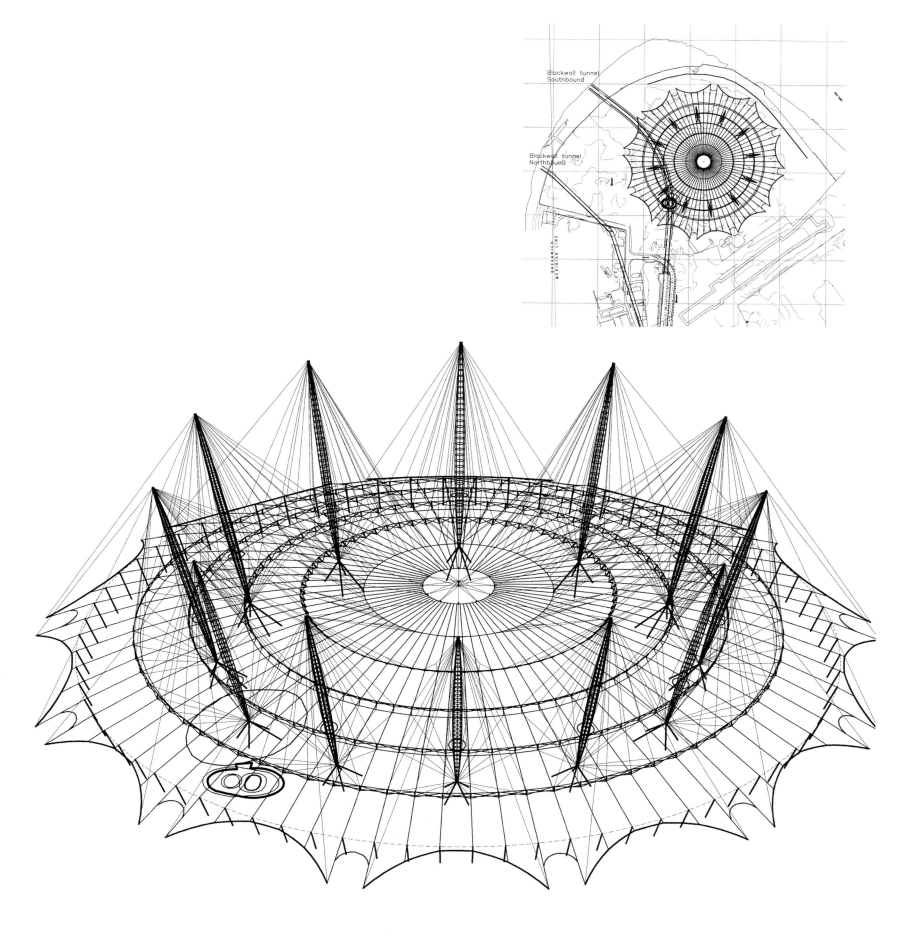

The Dome's twelve steel lattice masts, piercing through the Teflon-coated membrane roof, support a complicated arrangement of steel cables.

DYNAMIC EARTH CENTRE

ARCHITECT
Hopkins Architects, London (UK)

LOCATION
Canongate, Edinburgh (UK)

STRUCTURAL ENGINEER
Arup, London (UK)

CLIENT
Dynamic Earth Charitable Trust, Edinburgh (UK)

COMPLETION
1999

For this old brewery site in the Canongate neighbourhood of Edinburgh, the architects chose a PTFE-coated fibreglass membrane.

The Dynamic Earth Centre is positioned opposite Enric Miralles' 2004 Scottish Parliament building. In contrast to Miralles' metaphor of gently falling autumn leaves, Michael Hopkins' caterpillar is skewered to the ground with large pins. The tent canopy runs east–west, parallel to Edinburgh's Royal Mile. The site is the precise spot where James Hutton, the father of modern geology, lived and worked in the 18th century – there could hardly be a more suitable location. The centre uses interactive, virtual and wide-screen film technologies to simulate events in the Earth's evolution, from the Big Bang to the future of the planet. Visitors can experience earthquakes, volcanoes, and the various processes that formed natural settings, including that of Edinburgh.

Set against the rugged backdrop of Arthur's Seat and Salisbury Crags, the pavilion repeats the lines of the hilly countryside behind it. The centre appears more at ease with the harsh, natural surroundings of the city than with the city itself, and its luminous, billowing form strikes a counter note to the heavy, mounting formation of the Edinburgh cityscape. This luminosity is enhanced by the sheer glass walls that enclose it and advertise its welcoming presence at night. Four transparent skylights cross the fabric body where the supporting pairs of masts thrust through the roof. This same device was used at Hopkins' building for the Inland Revenue in Nottingham (1994), and avoids weakening the fabric cover by positioning the paired masts so that they do not penetrate the fabric directly. Instead, the masts slide through the skylight openings and focus attention on the dynamic interpenetration of the roof surface through these narrow slits.

The centre houses a globe-shaped multimedia cinema, located opposite the entrance and in line with the outdoor amphitheatre, along with a café and bar at either end, the latter with spiral stairs leading to the upper level. Its programme was more easily accommodated than that at Nottingham, and secondary canopies around the sides have been dispensed with, leaving a much simpler structure. Each pair of tubular steel masts is tilted outwards and carries steel-rod connections between the mast and the welded steel ladder girder. These tubular girders are stabilized from below by counter rods, and the frames are covered externally by trapezium-shaped panes of toughened safety glass, point fixed. The PTFE-coated fibreglass fabric roof, which extends out as far as the upright cantilevered glazed façade, has the same gentle anticlastic saddles, supported between open lozenge-shaped skylights. This is a particularly tricky detail since the membrane must be allowed to move in three dimensions. A membrane hinge bridges the gap between the roof edge and the glazed façade and absorbs movement in the roof, while a light membrane extends past the façade to the perimeter columns, anchored to the ground by steel-rod guys.

At the entrance, visitors are greeted by a fly-canopy which projects forward of the tent front. Tents, one hardly need repeat, are not fixed objects, and, in keeping with this, the Dynamic Earth Centre has a restless quality, much like the trees of Great Birnam Wood that marched to Dunsinane. Compared to the brooding quality of the buildings around it, this somewhat royal tent refuses to be cut off from the Edinburgh landscape.

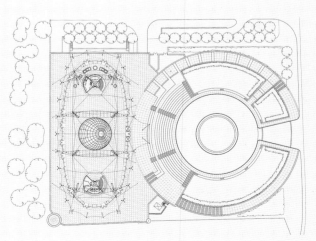

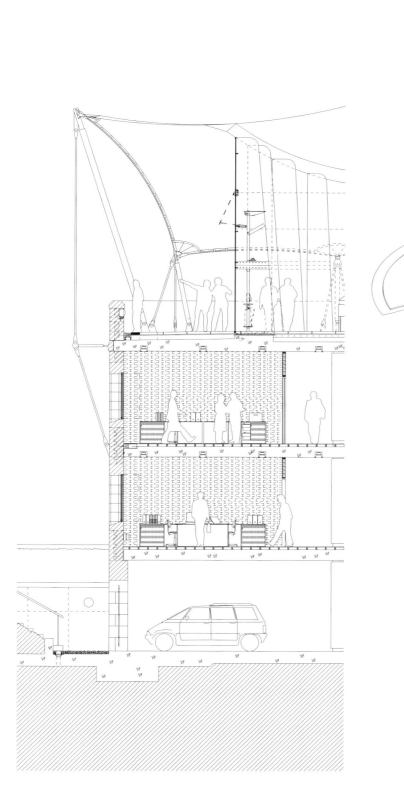

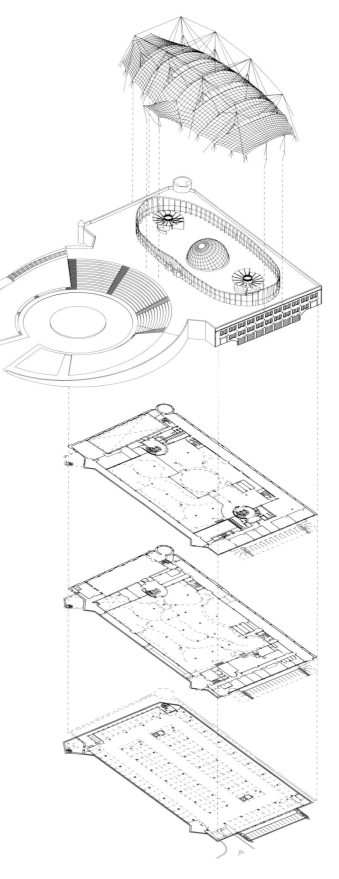

The outwardly tilted masts carry steel-rod connections between the masts and the tubular ladder girders, which are stabilized from below by counter rods.

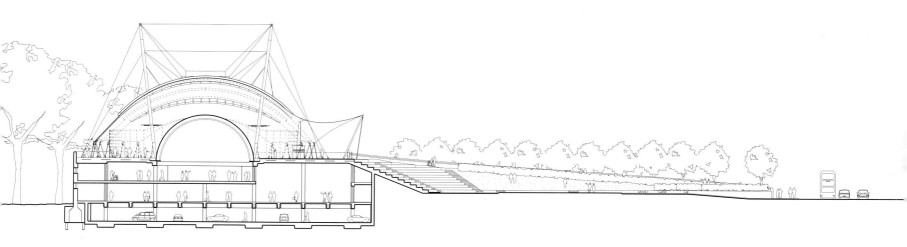

RINGS AND CONVERTIBLES

Not only did the Roman amphitheatre anticipate the modern sports arena, its large shade roof, or *vela* – the first instance of a fabric roof that was also convertible – also rivalled today's super-tent membrane. By virtue of its shape, the amphitheatre possessed an in-built compression ring ready-made to restrain lightweight, demountable fabric roofs. The majority of contemporary ring-cable roof structures have a similar arrangement of radial cables anchored to a rigid compression ring of masts around the periphery. Such roofs comprise a primary structure made of sealed, self-anchored compression and tension rings, braced by cables, with a prestressed fabric or cable-net roof stretched in between. Their lightness makes them superior to any truss structure. Similarly, convertible or retractable roofs take advantage of the ease of folding fabric. They are, in effect, tents, which (rather like an umbrella) can be opened when it rains and folded up again when the sun comes out. The mechanical extension and retraction of convertible roofs is automated by suspending the membrane from cable tractors that travel along cables. This type of roof exploits the basic properties of fabric: its natural flexibility and lightness.

Waldstadion, Frankfurt am Main (Germany). Von Gerkan, Marg & Partner, architects.

LA CARTUJA OLYMPIC STADIUM

ARCHITECT
Cruz y Ortiz, Seville (Spain)

LOCATION
La Cartuja, Seville (Spain)

ENGINEER
Schlaich Bergermann, Stuttgart (Germany)

CLIENT
Sociedad Estadio Olímpico de Sevilla,
Seville (Spain)

COMPLETION
1999

It comes as no surprise that football matches generate mass emotion, and in recent years the sport has been the cause of violent demonstrations and sublimated warfare. Supporters of opposing teams regularly clash in what has been interpreted as modern tribal behaviour. This has in turn led to the demand to place spectators as close as possible to the playing field, with the result that stands have moved ever closer to the players on the pitch.

The Olympic Stadium at La Cartuja was included in the city of Seville's prospective bids to host the Summer Olympics in 2004 (ultimately held in Athens) and in 2008 (Beijing). The stadium has occasionally been used as a venue for the Spanish national football team, and in 1999 provided the setting for the IAAF World Championships in Athletics. It has a 40m-deep oval roof, on axes of 275m x 229m, which covers an octagonal stand with seating for over 57,000 spectators. The roof itself has an 8m-deep outer compression ring tied to an inner tension ring-cable by cable trusses, and sits on eight supports. Instead of the customary suspender cables, the PVC membrane is supported by two sets of upper and lower cables, stabilized by vertical struts. The radial cables are connected by folded, plate-like membranes, whose valley folds deepen towards the outer compression ring.

The membrane used here at the Olympic Stadium at La Cartuja is a PVC-coated fabric, covering an area of 27,000m².

Despite not having a permanent role, the stadium has hosted major sporting events, including the 1999 IAAF World Championships in Athletics and the 2003 UEFA Cup Final.

ALLIANZ ARENA

ARCHITECT
Herzog & de Meuron Architekten, Basel (Switzerland), with Alpine Bau Deutschland, Eching (Germany)

LOCATION
Fröttmaning, Munich (Germany)

ENGINEER
Ingenieurbüro R + R, Munich (Germany)

CLIENT
HypoVereinsbank, Munich (Germany)

COMPLETION
2005

From a distance, the new Allianz Arena – nicknamed the 'bird's nest' – looks like a large, overturned albino tractor tyre, with its rhomboid pillows repeating the deeply grooved pattern of tyre treads. It looks smaller than it actually is because the rounded shape minimizes the visual impact of the massive 50m-high, 258m-long and 227m-wide structure. The inflated ETFE-pillow roof and walls in fact protect over 60,000 spectators, while dedicated spaces for VIPs are hidden away in eight-storey, double-glazed office spaces, separated from the general areas behind the outer pillow cover.

Nearly 3,000 rhomboid inflated pillows, with a total surface area of 64,000m², were required for the outside walls and roof. On the outside, the stadium tilts outwards from its base and then ascends in a slow arc over the top, continuing on over three tiers of seating ramps. The pillows are fixed to a lattice grid of galvanized hollow steel sections, which are in-filled by two-layer ETFE membrane elements on extruded aluminium sections. A regulating facility adjusts the pressure of the conditioned (dry) air in the individual pillows to meet changing loads from wind.

The transparency of the membrane also varies: in many areas it is transparent, while in others it is translucent white. The ETFE foil can also be illuminated in the resident football clubs' (Bayern Munich and TSV 1860 Munich) colours of red, white and blue, or changed in the space of two minutes to avoid creating a highway hazard to passing motor traffic. The 0.2mm-thick ETFE membrane is up to 98 per cent UV-permeable. Pressure sensors measure snow-load and cause the pressure to increase to balance out the load. Each pillow has a surface area of 35m².

A partially retractable sun-shading system has been installed with both reflecting and sound-absorbing qualities to handle solar radiation. The ETFE membrane is fireproof and self-cleaning, and can be damaged only when attacked directly with a knife or, more dramatically, a missile.

As a host venue for the 2006 World Cup, this new football stadium is a prominent landmark on the northern edge of Munich. In 1972, Frei Otto's anti-monumental cable-net roofs for the Munich Olympic Games presented a new democratic image of West Germany under the chancellorship of Willy Brandt. Thirty-three years on, the nearby Allianz Arena has once again put the sporting world's media spotlight back on Munich, with a revised and updated, if more obese, image.

The ETFE membrane covering 'Europe's most modern stadium' lights up in colours that change according to which home team is playing at the time.

WALDSTADION

ARCHITECT
Von Gerkan, Marg & Partner,
Hamburg (Germany)

LOCATION
Frankfurt am Main (Germany)

ENGINEER
Schlaich Bergermann, Stuttgart (Germany)

COMPLETION
2005

The new Waldstadion, a redesign by Von Gerkan, Marg & Partner of the existing 1925 stadium for the 2006 World Cup (see also Allianz Arena, p. 130), is the largest convertible roof in the world. Around the outside, the stadium (now known officially as the Commerzbank-Arena) has a combined, fixed membrane roof covering the stands, with an almost rectangular convertible roof filling the opening over the playing field.

This combination necessitated an arrangement of two inner tension rings, spread apart by vertical struts 60.65m in from the outer compression ring. The roof over the stands is fixed to the lower cable and slopes down, following the rake of the two-tiered stand. The two spread tension rings 'float' above the playing field and the central node that holds them together, and serves as the primary structure for a 78.7m x 122.72m retractable roof. The convertible membrane withdraws into a node above the centre of the pitch, from which is suspended the video cube used to film aerial images of the match in progress.

The outer compression ring is supported by forty-four columns rising to the top of the stand. Though more rounded, this ring is almost identical in shape to the two inner tension rings. The translucent PTFE-coated fibreglass membrane is fixed to the lower forty-four radial cables of the cable girders, and becomes a polycarbonate roof sheath in the forward section to ensure better lighting of the playing field. When fully deployed, the two roofs slope to a gutter at the inner edge of the fixed membrane canopy.

At this World Cup stadium in Frankfurt, PTFE-coated fibreglass was used for the outer membrane, and polycarbonate sheeting for the inner convertible roof. The total area is 9,658m².

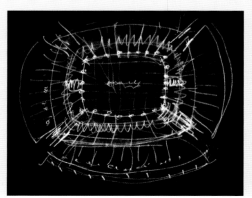

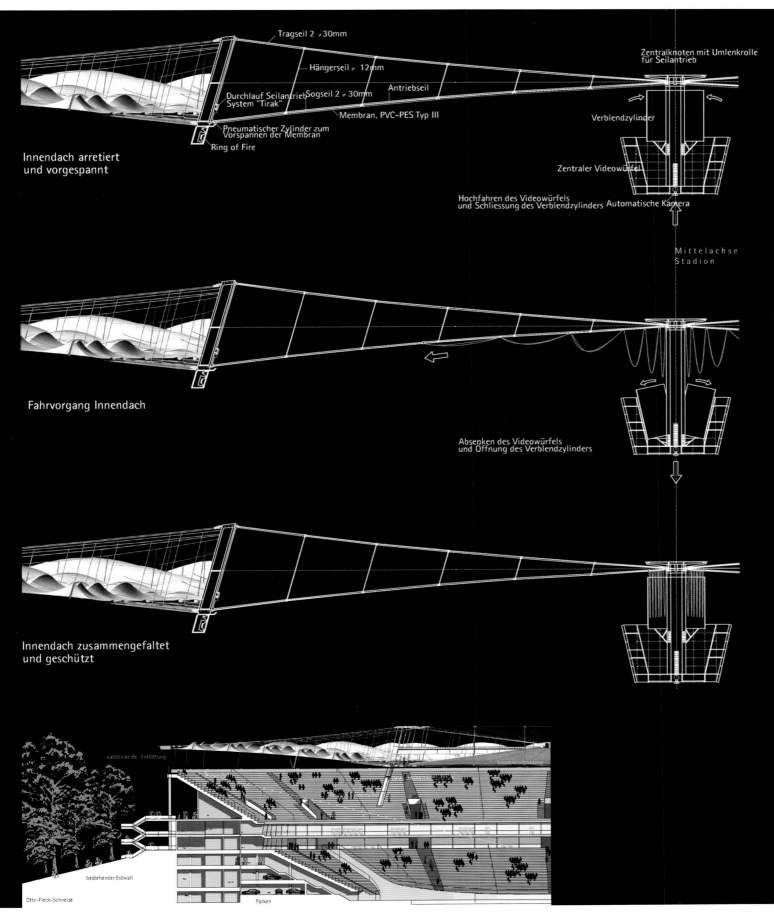

Innendach arretiert
und vorgespannt

Tragseil 2 ⌀30mm

Hängerseil ⌀ 12mm

Sogseil 2 ⌀ 30mm   Antriebseil

Durchlauf Seilantrieb
System "Tirak"

Membran, PVC-PES Typ III

Pneumatischer Zylinder zum
Vorspannen der Membran

Ring of Fire

Zentralknoten mit Umlenkrolle
für Seilantrieb

Verblendzylinder

Zentraler Videowürfel

Hochfahren des Videowürfels
und Schliessung des Verblendzylinders   Automatische Kamera

Mittelachse
Stadion

Fahrvorgang Innendach

Absenken des Videowürfels
und Öffnung des Verblendzylinders

Innendach zusammengefaltet
und geschützt

natürliche Be - Entlüftung

Sonneneinstrahlung

bestehender Erdwall

Otto-Fleck-Schneise

Parken

The stadium seats over 52,000 spectators and is the home of football team Eintracht Frankfurt. Television cameras are housed within a video cube suspended beneath the convertible membrane.

ARCHITECT
Silja Tillner, Vienna (Austria)

LOCATION
Vienna (Austria)

STRUCTURAL ENGINEER
Schlaich Bergermann, Stuttgart (Germany),
with Vasko & Partner, Vienna (Austria)

MEMBRANE CONSTRUCTION
Covertex, Obing (Germany)

STEEL CONSTRUCTION
Filzamer, Vienna (Austria)

CLIENT
City of Vienna (Austria)

COMPLETION
2000

Modern construction can often seem awkward and strange when placed against the historic fabric of a city: either the new emulates the old, or seeks invisibility by being minimal. Neither approach is entirely satisfactory. Frequently, the new work will lack any authentic connection with the historic structure, and invisibility is an impossible goal from the start.

Throughout history, tents have existed side-by-side with more conventional buildings. In the Middle East, they enhanced the vibrancy and colour of urban life by this accidental juxtaposition with the region's squares and *caravanserai* (roadside inns) and resulting frisson of lifestyles. But in perhaps no other city is the coexistence of tents with palaces more apt than in Vienna, which survived successive sieges by Ottoman forces in 1529 and, for the last time, in 1683. Vienna has a unique tent legacy not seen in other European capitals, and the insertion of a retractable parallel wave membrane into Vienna's town hall courtyard continues this long tradition.

Frei Otto liked to call the inversion of a hanging chain into an upright position the 'Indian rope trick'. Antonio Gaudí also exploited this swift conversion of a shape from pure tension to pure compression, which underlined the generic identity of purely stressed tensile and compression forms. This similarity explains the success of this particular fabric roof in the courtyard of Vienna's *Rathaus*. With wonderful simplicity, like a complex melody in several parts, the fabric waves of the roof counterpoint the graceful stone profiles of the hall's arcade.

The courtyard is used for public events, and thus requires protection from the weather. Previously, a large marquee had been erected as a temporary shelter, but there was a good deal that was unsatisfactory with the arrangement: it was clumsy and slow to erect; the masts intruded on the space; and there was no provision for dealing with rainwater. Worst of all was its lack of sympathy with the neo-Gothic architecture of the town hall. Silja Tillner's new roof provides a permanent fabric cover for the courtyard that can be extended at any time over a large portion of it, leaving the space open to the sky with a folded fabric that echoes the profile of the masonry arcade arches. Movable downpipes at the ends of the canopy valleys convey rainwater to drains at ground level.

The structure, which is mounted on the walls on each side of the court, comprises fixed-edge beams that support tracks, along which the roof moves. The four triangular-section inverted bowstring trusses relieve the masonry walls of the horizontal tensile loads that would otherwise bear on them. Motors at each end of the front truss either pull or push the fabric roof into position. The fabric ridges are carried on cables fixed to movable tracks, which are dragged into position by the moving front truss with the valley cables secured and anchored at each side by chains extending inside thin downpipes over drainage holes in the paving. These tensile drainage anchors have to be manually disconnected and reconnected each time the roof is extended or retracted.

The marriage here between masonry and fabric, old and new, is consummated with refined grace. Though each may seem entirely opposed and different, their juxtaposition, like that of compression with tensile forms, produces a wonderful frisson.

A translucent polyester membrane was used to construct the 100m² canopy for the courtyard of this historic building.

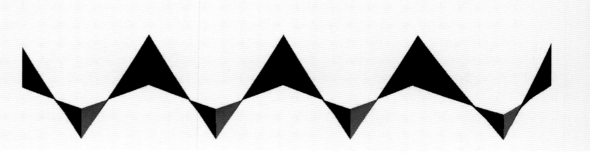

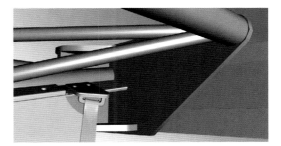
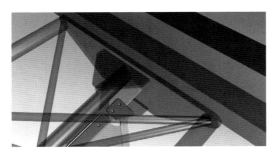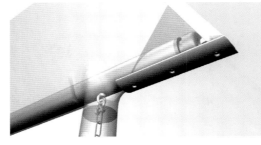
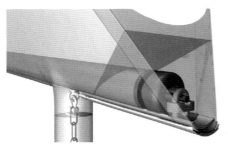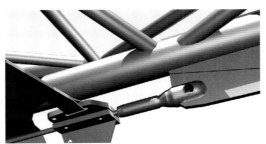
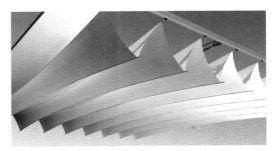
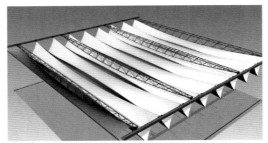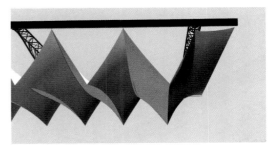

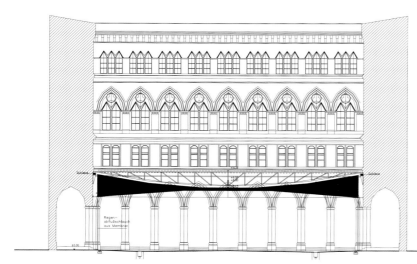

In a harmonious pairing of old and new, the wave-like fabric roof complements, rather than competes with, the town hall's graceful neo-Gothic arcade.

ARCHITECT
Planinghaus Architekten,
Darmstadt (Germany)

LOCATION
Duisburg (Germany)

CONSULTING ENGINEER
Schlaich Bergermann, Stuttgart (Germany)

FABRICATOR
Vector-Foiltec, Bremen (Germany)

CLIENT
Landschaftspark Duisburg-Nord,
Duisburg (Germany)

COMPLETION
2003

The Ruhr region has been famous for its heavy industry and steel production from the 19th century until recently, when closures severely affected the local economy. The closure in 1985 of the Duisburg-Meiderich smelting works left 500 acres of industrial wasteland, and an international building show at Emscher Park was consequently held to draw attention the plight of the old plant. Large industrial steel plants can be difficult to assimilate successfully into the urban landscape, but with a little imagination blast furnaces, gasometers, steam blowers and foundry halls can be turned into wonderful sculptures. The challenge is to find suitable uses which do not require new construction that is either inappropriate or false.

'Celebration not demolition' is the theme of Peter Latz's industrial Land Art approach for the masterplan of Landschaftspark Duisburg-Nord. The strong industrial structures were kept and given new uses under a policy of minimum intervention and natural regeneration of the site. The cast house of furnace no. 1 (one of three) has been resurrected as a theatre, while next to it, the Piazza Metallica stage for concerts and theatrical performances includes a collage of steel plates from the foundry pits. Industrial elements such as chimneys, gantries, girders, metal tunnels and chutes are illuminated at night in green, blue and red strip-lighting.

The theatre's open-air foyer and exposed auditorium seating is protected by Planinghaus Architekten's convertible roof, which runs along parallel wave-like tracks. The roof can assume three different positions: over the stage, over the exposed seating, and fully extended over the foyer. It consists of nine 24m-long, 3m-wide inflated ETFE membrane pillows that are suspended from linked 'cushion' dollies, with each pillow supported along its edge by 1.3m-deep spiral steel-cable stiffening trusses between the two tracks.

The pillow shape is maintained by internal air pressure, which can be topped up as needed with air pumped from a static source beside the blast furnace. The air supply is routed along an energy duct to the pneumatic beams. These freely curved tracks extend from the foundry hall to the open-air foyer, and avoid the existing service ducts. Outside the foundry hall, the undulating 500/25mm steel tracks are supported on two V-shaped pairs of 300/10mm tubular steel columns on either side, fixed to existing refurbished footings of the former crane track. Within the hall, the tracks are mounted on the shed portal structure. The convertible roof, a modest 570m², is driven by synchronized electric motors on the first pneumatic beam dolly, much like carriages being pulled along a railway line by a locomotive. The motors drive the roof through a rack-and-pinion system of toothed rods fixed to the track carriages.

The old and new parts are clearly distinguished to avoid confusion about which is which: the hall is ponderous and heavy, whilst the new travelling roof is transparent and delicate. This is helped by the honest expression of the structural functions of the new convertible pillow roof and the foundry hall. Neither one competes for our attention. Each is a true structural statement: the roof acquiesces and allows the old plant to dominate.

The foil pillow roof was constructed from a two-layer Texlon ETFE membrane. From inside the cast house, it pushes out on tracks to protect the foyer during inclement weather.

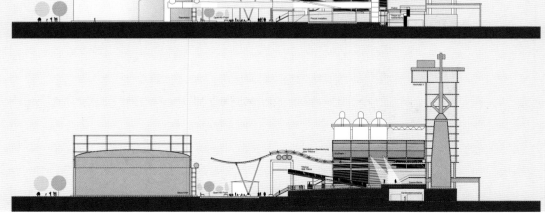

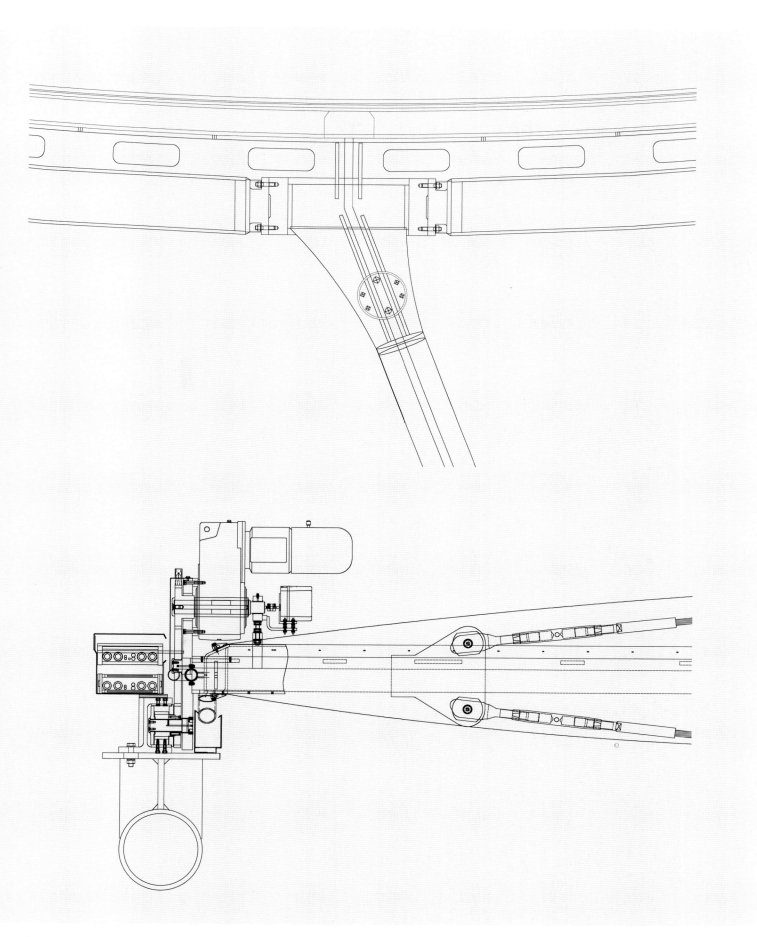

Peter Latz's masterplan carefully preserved the park's industrial past, while the architects' innovative roof introduced a contemporary savour.

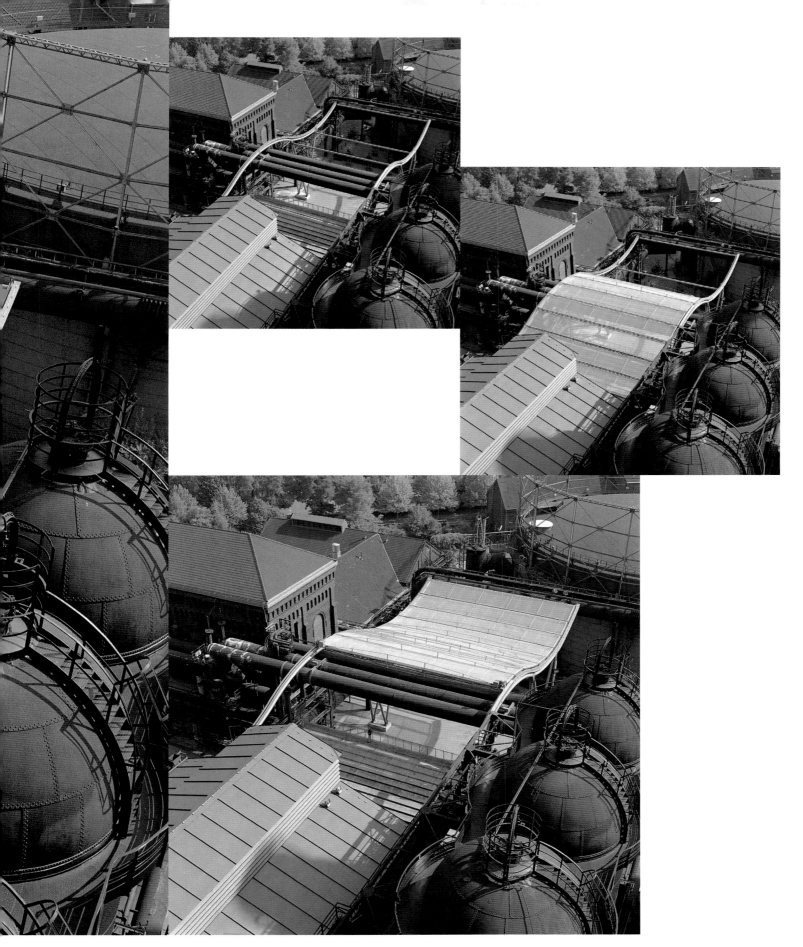

ARCHITECT
ASP Schweger Assoziierte Architekten,
Hamburg (Germany)

LOCATION
Rothenbaum, Hamburg (Germany)

ENGINEER
Sobek + Rieger, Stuttgart (Germany)

CLIENT
Deutscher Tennis Bund, Hamburg (Germany)

COMPLETION
1997

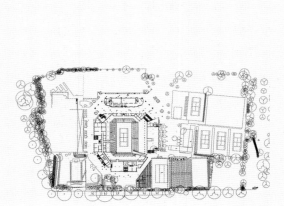

The PVC-coated polyester fabric used
for the convertible roof has anti-
adhesive properties to ensure that
it is self-cleaning.

To ensure that televised play can continue in all weathers, venues for important tennis competitions have increasingly found it necessary to provide flexibly covered or enclosed courts, and the Rothenbaum tennis stadium is no exception. Its combination of a fixed, radially cable-supported outer membrane with a radially retractable inner membrane roof, however, is unusual. The free-span structure is a typical ring-stadium type; what makes it different is the 63m-diameter inner roof, which covers an area of 3,000m². The asymmetrical roof has been designed to avoid casting shadows over the court and the faces of serving players, and with a transparent, self-cleaning membrane canopy around the outside of the stadium.

The outer fixed roof spans between an outer compression ring and an inner hollow hub. Thirty-six upper and lower spokes connect the compression ring to the hub, which has eighteen suspended masts connected at the top and bottom of outwardly tilted masts. The outer roof has a high-point geometry cut out of torispherical heads, with the shell-like fabric elements clamped to their edges. The PVC-coated polyester membrane of both roofs is fixed to the lower cable spokes, so that the cables are concealed from inside. These incline in opposite directions to allow rainwater to drain into a ring-shaped, translucent gutter.

The movement of the inner roof is automatically controlled by sensors. The membrane folds and unfolds as it travels towards and away from the central hub, and the bunched fabric hangs loosely in the fully retracted state. Broad, high-tensile strength bands were inserted into the membrane to contend with forces produced by the movement

of cable tractors pulling it along the radial suspension cables. At the hub, specially designed pockets protect the bunched membrane folds from tearing or rotting. An overlapping apron, weighted by chain links, was inserted between the radial cables to drain off rainwater from the inner to the outer roof.

Ordinarily, tents are erected and struck in stages to avoid damage to the tent cloth and to ensure that the membrane is adequately tensioned. In a convertible roof, this is done automatically and must be perfectly synchronized to avoid tearing, particularly during the extension phase. Great precision is required during the pre-tensioning of the membrane, so that the inserted bands do their job well and allow the mechanical unfolding of the membrane to happen at maximum speed. The unfolding action is a critical time: the longer it takes, the more likely wind, or some other effect, will cause a problem. The extension of the membrane, therefore, needs to be swift and smooth. For this reason, in practice, the calculation of the pre-tensioning forces must be extremely precise.

Visually, the unfurling of a convertible roof resembles a slow-motion Disney animation of a flower opening. What makes it more impressive is the effect of light on the translucent membrane: against the sunlit sky each layer of fabric adds its shadow, increasing the layering effect and enchantment to the event. In much the same way that the iris of the human eye dilates to manage the amount of light, a convertible roof also controls the quality of light entering the stadium. The Rothenbaum stadium, too, is a combination of physical grace, strength and flexibility, uniting the benefits of both fixed and convertible roofs.

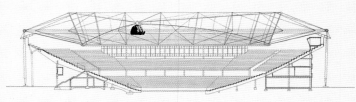

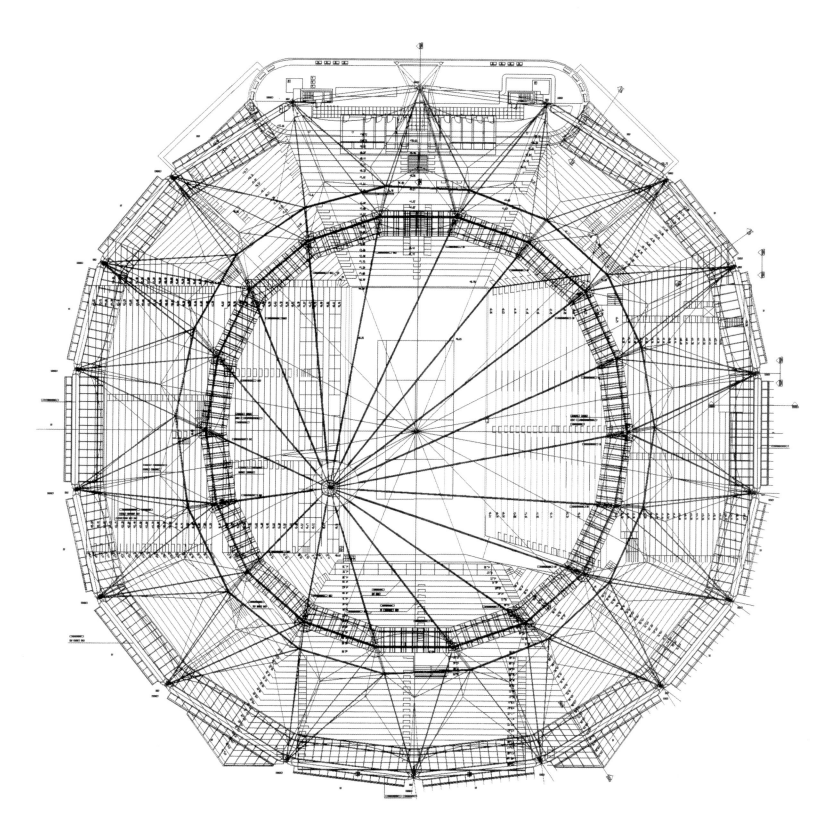

This tennis stadium, one of the oldest in Europe and the largest in Germany, has been given a spectacular convertible roof that unfurls like a flower opening in the sun.

ATRIUM COVERS, FABRIC WALLS

Atrium covers, modern versions of the *vela* roofs of Ancient Rome can be seen around the world today, particularly in northern Europe, where the long winters encourage the covering of outdoor spaces while simultaneously seeking to retain a connection with natural daylight. They can be small and intimate, or large and intimidating: the conical roof for the Sony Centre (p. 162) in Berlin, for example, is much larger than the fixed atrium roof of the Yapi Kredi Operations Centre (p. 158) near Istanbul, but pales in comparison next to the Munich Airport Centre at 19,000m^2. Such roofs avoid the expense of providing ground anchorage points, but attaching a membrane to an existing building with guy cables can prove troublesome. Fabric walls, on the other hand, are structurally independent, but are much less common. A spectacular example, however, is the 320m-high, double-layer PTFE-coated membrane wall of the Burj Al Arab Hotel (p. 170) in Dubai, while at the smaller end of the spectrum is Hopkins Architects' Wildscreen-at-Bristol (p. 166). But whatever their size, atrium covers and fabric roofs all have one thing in common: their ability to modify an environment without entirely excluding the outside.

Wildscreen-at-Bristol, Bristol (UK).
Hopkins Architects.

ARCHITECT
John McAslan & Partners, London (UK)

LOCATION
Gebze, near Istanbul (Turkey)

ASSOCIATE ARCHITECT
Metex Design Group, Istanbul (Turkey)

ENGINEER
Arup, Istanbul (Turkey)

MEMBRANE FABRICATOR
Koch-Hightex, Rimsting (Germany)

CLIENT
Yapi ve Kredi Bankasi, Istanbul (Turkey)

COMPLETION
1997

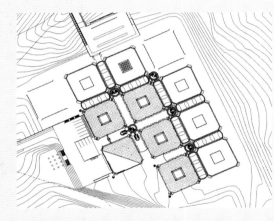

A PTFE-coated woven fibreglass membrane, 900 gsm weight with 13 per cent translucency, was used in this delicate construction.

Light plays an important role in Ottoman architecture. This traditional concern has been updated by the fabric roofs of the Yapi Kredi Bank Centre at Gebze, extensions of the traditional Roman *vela*. The roofs shelter and protect the street, while effecting a wonderful sense of the outside. The steeply sloping site in Gebze, some 50km southeast of Istanbul, overlooks the Sea of Marmara on the Asian side of the Bosphorus.

The complex comprises ten independent atrium-shaped blocks, linked by a circulation grid of covered streets. The arrangement of the blocks was a response to the bank's need for a flexible, easily adaptable environment that at the same time ensured a high level of security. Turkey is a notorious earthquake region, and the bank is situated in an area of high seismic risk (corresponding to UBC Zone 4). Consequently, the structure was designed to withstand minor earthquakes. Lightweight tents are much less vulnerable to earthquakes than heavy masonry construction, as witnessed by the destruction in 2003 of the ancient mud-brick citadel of Bam, in Iran. Fabric roofs are lightweight, which eliminates a critical factor in earthquakes.

The internal streets are discontinuous; each is ended by cylindrical glass-block stairs at each intersection. Like their Roman counterparts, the main function of the fabric roofs is shade, while still allowing sufficient daylight to reach down into the partly planted pedestrian streets. Lightweight roof trusses were placed across the covered streets, consisting of pairs of arches that lean outwards from a common springing point at each end in a lemon-wedge configuration. The PTFE-coated woven fibreglass fabric stretches over and rests on these tilted, light tubular arches,

and is only restrained at the end arches abutting the stair and lift towers. These end arches are more complicated than their counterparts, and involve a third arch which is laid horizontally and linked to the outer upright arch using inclined tubes that double as glazing bar supports. The end arch is mounted on spherical bearings that allow it to rock about in both the X- and Y-axes. The longitudinal tensions from the street roof are resisted by cables anchored directly to the building façades, one storey below. The intermediate paired arches are pivoted about a single axis and are stabilized against movements by a Y-shaped lever. Its function is to counterbalance movement in the fabric by a series of ties to the end arches. The fabric was installed with a prestress of 4kN/m, a fraction of the fabric's ultimate strip tensile strength of 85kN/m. Under characteristic wind-loads, the tensile stress rises to 16kN/m.

As so often occurs in membrane structures, the critical point was the junction of the roof with the main building under wind deformations of up to 20cm. The movement of the roof was dealt with by an attached skirt, which was turned back on itself by the inclusion of uniformly spaced plastic battens. These battens were sized and tensioned to hold the fabric in place while allowing the necessary movement. The cabled fabric roof edges oversail the cantilevered glass strips fixed directly to the building, which isolate the roof and cause it to appear to float above the street below.

SONY CENTRE

ARCHITECT
Murphy/Jahn Architects, Chicago, Illinois (USA)

LOCATION
Potzdamer Platz, Berlin (Germany)

PROJECT DEVELOPER
Tishman Speyer Properties, Berlin (Germany)

ENGINEER
Arup, New York, New York (USA)

MEMBRANE FABRICATOR
Birdair, Amherst, New York (USA)

ROOF SUBCONTRACTOR
Waagner-Biro, Vienna (Austria)

CLIENT
Sony Deutschland, Berlin (Germany)

COMPLETION
2000

For all its huge size, the roof for Sony's European headquarters on the western edge of Potzdamer Platz is still a modern *vela*. But Berlin is not Rome: the daylight is less intense and the roof must be a shield against snow. Engineer Ross Clarke of Arup suggested the idea for a tilted hyperbolic roof to the architects at their first meeting in 1992. Pressed by Helmut Jahn, Clarke cited the conical roof covers he had designed for eight huge grain silos on South Australia's Yorke Peninsula. Slicing the silo roofs at 8° had created an elongated plan that fitted the ellipse formed within the buildings around the triangular city block. The result in Berlin was a tilted cone of impressive dimensions: 102m on the main axis and 78m on the minor axis, with a 42.5m kingpost in the middle to prop up the inclined umbrella canopy.

The giant roof is the centrepiece of the project: around it are seven buildings that range in height from 40m to 100m, with a gross floor area of 212,000m². The roof structure is a simple bicycle wheel, comprising two radial layers of cables forming the spokes. The cables, which connect the elliptical rim on the outside edge to a tilted axle at the centre, generate a series of alternating ridges and valleys radiating out from the roof crown. The objective of the roof is, in short, to extend the use of the plaza during inclement weather and to satisfy the requirements for ventilation and daylighting. Although Jahn was keen to avoid a similar shape to Norman Foster's Reichstag dome nearby, there is an almost uncanny resemblance, especially to the Reichstag's inverted glass dagger. The mixed glass-and-fabric solution is similar to another Murphy/Jahn project, the 19,000m² forum roof of the Munich Airport Centre. A defect of such fabric

roofs in general is the blandness of the light and the lack of contrast and interest within the space. In addition, fabric structures require only 15 per cent of their area as evenly distributed openings to provide sufficient daylight below. For the Sony Centre, this dictated the use of Teflon-coated fibreglass, with a translucency of 17.5 per cent, as an additional material for part of the roof.

Assuming a minimal or soap-film surface, the form-finding procedure followed multiple steps: firstly, for a uniform prestress; secondly, the cables were assumed to have stiffness; and thirdly, stiffness and self-weight were assumed in all the structural elements and calculations were undertaken on this model. In plan, an angle of 10° was finally selected for one fabric valley element. Each element was separated by a laminated glass panel (2mm x 8mm), with the fabric ending two-thirds of the way up, short of the apex, and the glazing completing the roof above the tops of the fabric valley blades. The connection of the glass panels to the radial cables presented a challenge. Arup initially designed stainless-steel bearings with sliding joints and ceramic washers, but later elastomeric buffers were substituted that allowed the glass to float above the structure.

Despite the obvious simplicity of the bicycle-wheel structure, a great deal of subtlety has been introduced to make it a far more enticing object than might otherwise have been the case. The Sony forum acts as a powerful urban focus in an unquestionably important area of Berlin. If its shape is more strongly geometric than other fabric roofs, this does not make it any less effective and even, with its mixture of transparent and translucent glass and fabric panels that sparkle and contrast in the daylight, adds to its sculptural intrigue.

Sheerfill V (a Teflon-coated woven fibreglass) by Chemfab was used as the material for this forum roof.

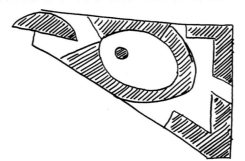

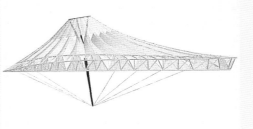

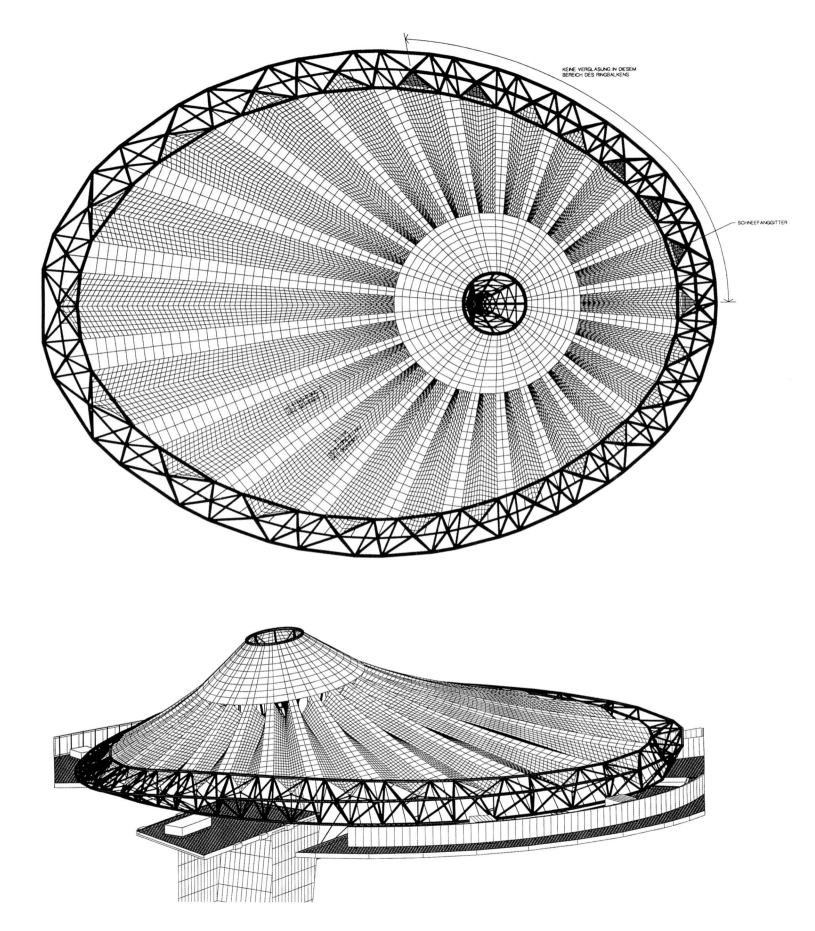

KEINE VERGLASUNG IN DIESEM
BEREICH DES RINGBALKENS

SCHNEEFANGGITTER

The roof shape was generated by a tilted hyperbolic cone on an ellipse. Two upward-curved ridge cables and one downward-curved valley cable frame a single roof unit, which is held in equilibrium by its geometry in space and its prestress conditions within the elements.

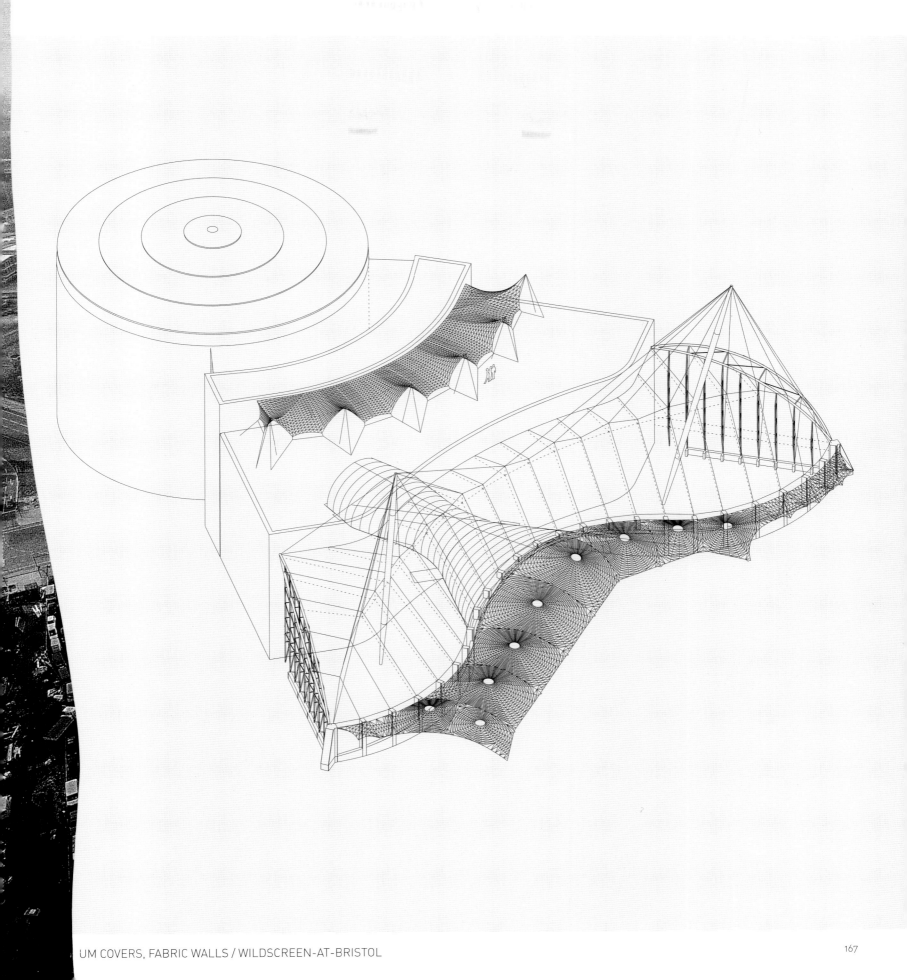

UM COVERS, FABRIC WALLS / WILDSCREEN-AT-BRISTOL

ARCHITECT
W.S. Atkins Overseas, Dubai (United Arab Emirates)

LOCATION
Dubai (United Arab Emirates)

ENGINEERS
Al Habtoor Engineering, Abu Dhabi (United Arab Emirates); Fletcher Construction, Auckland (New Zealand); Murray & Roberts, Bedfordview (South Africa)

MEMBRANE FABRICATOR
Skyspan, Rimsting (Germany)

CLIENT
HH General Sheikh Mohammed bin Rashid Al Maktoum (United Arab Emirates)

COMPLETION
2004

The two-layer, PTFE-coated fibreglass membrane used for the Burj Al Arab Hotel offered a number of structural advantages.

At 321m, the Burj Al Arab is one of the tallest hotels in the world, exceeded only by the 333m-high Rose Tower (completed in 2007), also in Dubai. The world's first 'seven-star' hotel, it is also one of the most luxurious and spectacular in a region where luxury is a commonplace. Built on a man-made island just off the coast, the tower can be seen from all sides. And much like the Sydney Opera House, it is an impressive sculptural object, surrounded by the waters of the Arabian Gulf. Its enormous fabric wall is a deliberate reference to the billowing sail of lateen-rigged Arab *dhows*, but instead of one there are two long, tapering yards, one for each side. And instead of the customary triangular lateen sail slung diagonally across the mast, these two curving arms rise vertically over the top and meet the mast behind the tower.

The hotel plan is an open V closed by an impressive translucent, double-layer membrane façade that creates a full-height atrium space, which, like everything to do with the hotel, was meant to set a record (in this case, as the world's largest atrium; the twin 152m-high towers at the west front of Cologne cathedral would easily fit inside it). To achieve such exceptional height and lightness, a series of challenging structural conditions – related to wind conditions and the expansion and contraction of the membrane due to the wide variations in temperature – had to be met. The individual membrane panels are supported by twelve horizontal ribs, spaced at 14m centres vertically. The low weight per square metre resulted in savings in the weight of steel.

Some 7,500m^2 of membrane and liner were required for the wall. Because the façade faces south, only 2 to 3 per cent transparency was necessary to naturally illuminate the atrium.

PTFE membranes are UV-resistant, non-combustible, and have a high reflectance. The smooth membrane surface self-cleans every time it rains, and normally does not require further cleaning. The life expectancy of the material is in excess of thirty years, more than adequate for most commercial applications. Lighting can be used at night to change the membrane colour from white to yellow, green, violet or red, or combinations of the above. The top and bottom can be different colours (red top, blue bottom), and there are many other possibilities, such as yellow–violet or red–green combinations, to enliven the night scene.

ATRIUM COVERS, FABRIC WALLS / BURJ AL ARAB HOTEL

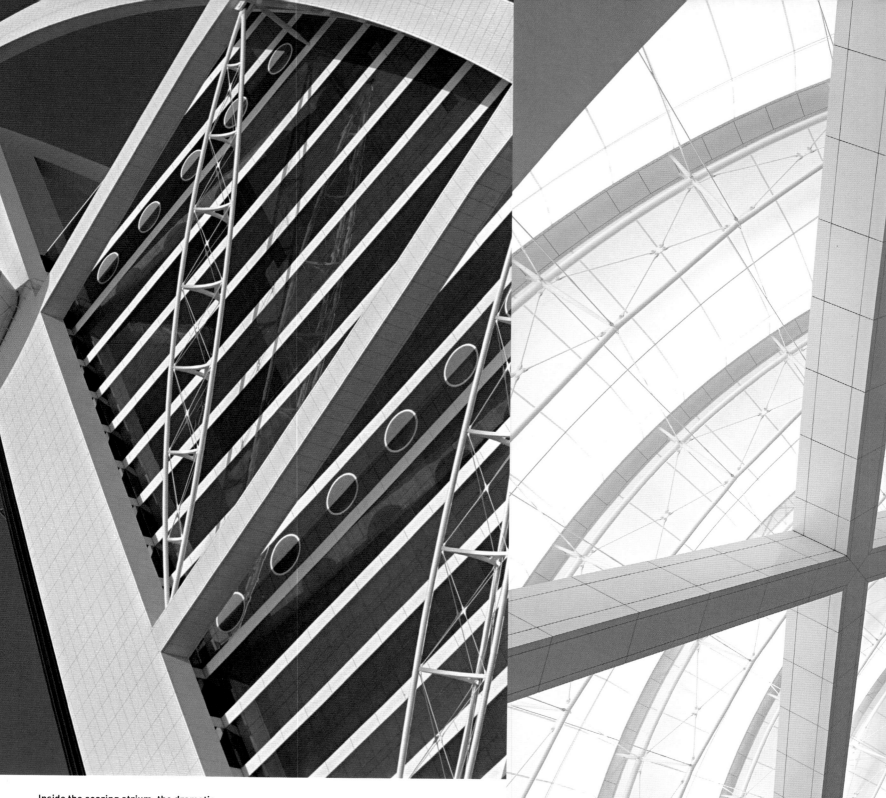

Inside the soaring atrium, the dramatic beauty of the enormous fabric wall – in itself a sculptural achievement of striking monumentality – can be seen to full effect.

ATRIUM COVERS, FABRIC WALLS / BURJ AL ARAB HOTEL

NEW INTERPRETATIONS

From grid shells to bubble wrap, new materials and shapes are paving the way for a revolution in the way membranes are used in architecture. The grid shell (seen to stunning effect at Shigeru Ban's Japanese Pavilion for Expo 2000; p. 178) was pioneered by Frei Otto in 1962 as the result of his research into spatial deformation of lattices for domes. Unlike Buckminster Fuller's spherical geodesic domes, grid shells come in an almost limitless range of organic shapes. But despite their economy and flexibility, few have been built to date. ETFE cushions, however, have been used to cover a number of recent projects, including the Eden Project (p. 184) in Cornwall and the Water Cube (p. 190), built for the 2008 Olympic Games in Beijing. ETFE-inflated pillows can be used in combination with other sheathing materials, and can solve problems of fixing and detailing, as well as (except in tight corners) looking beautiful and smooth. Following the example of installation artist Christo, fabric has been used to create extraordinary artworks that challenge what we mean by membrane structures. Dominik Baumüller's Rotational Pneu (p. 196) is a delightful conjuring trick, driven more by imagination than by practical concerns. Many a serious invention has started in this way.

The Water Cube, Beijing (China).
PTW Architects.

JAPANESE PAVILION, EXPO 2000

ARCHITECT
Shigeru Ban, Tokyo (Japan)

LOCATION
Hanover (Germany)

PROJECT TEAM
Shigeru Ban, Nobutaka Higara,
Shigeru Hiraki, Jun Yasaki

STRUCTURAL ENGINEER
Büro Happold, Berlin (Germany)

CONSULTANT
Frei Otto, Leonburg (Germany)

CONSTRUCTION
Takenaka Europe, Düsseldorf (Germany)

CLIENT
Japan External Trade Organization,
Berlin (Germany)

COMPLETION
2000

The membrane that covered this innovative cardboard structure was comprised of an inner layer of non-combustible paper, fibreglass fabric and polythene sheeting, and an outer layer of transparent PVC-coated polyester fabric.

Given that the theme for Expo 2000 was the environment and sustainable development, Shigeru Ban, famous for his cardboard-tube structures, was the natural choice to design the Japanese Pavilion. Not unexpectedly, Ban chose paper tubes as his basic structural element. And knowing of Frei Otto's work on grid shells, he asked Otto to act as consultant for the project.

The structure Ban proposed would produce a minimum of industrial waste at the Expo's conclusion. Based on his prior experience with emergency shelters for the UN High Commissioner for Refugees in Africa, he chose paper tubes made by Sonoco Europe. Ban's first thought was a tunnel arch of paper tubes, but concern about the high cost of timber joints caused him to reconsider. This led to the exploitation of a characteristic property of paper tubes, namely that they could be as long as he wished. The result was a 12m-high tunnel grid shell with no joints, measuring 72m long by 25m wide. Instead of a simple arch, Ban and Otto developed a three-dimensional curved grid shell with indentations in its height and width comprising three fused domes, which made it stronger against lateral strain. It would be the largest cardboard structure ever made.

Like all of Otto's previous grid shells, the Japanese Pavilion would be constructed flat and then gradually (over two weeks) jacked vertically to achieve its final shape. The 20m-long cardboard tubes, weighing 100kg each, were joined together by spigot connectors to produce a total length of 68m. Stiffening was achieved by thin, ladder-like timber arch trusses on the outside, stayed with wires perpendicular to the axis. The cover was a specially developed waterproof and fireproof

translucent (and recyclable) paper, which was reinforced by bonding it onto an inner transparent PVC membrane. The open ends were closed with the same material, supported by diagonal grids of cardboard stiffened with timber and connected to tubular steel nodes. At this stage, everything seemed set to proceed.

But the Hanover City Authority objected and the proof engineer was dismissed. Because the PVC in the membrane could not be recycled and gave off dioxins when it was burnt, an alternative membrane had to be found. Tokyo firm Taiyo Kogyo was enlisted and came up with 12cm-diameter tubes that easily passed the mandatory strength and B12 fireproof requirements at the first attempt. The testing of the paper glass-reinforced cover was more difficult, but ultimately satisfied the B12 requirement. The paper membrane was fixed using waterproof tape to battens stapled to the timber frames. Next, the city authorities demanded that the paper membrane be replaced by a conventional PVC membrane rated at B1, a fireproof grade higher. It was decided to place a transparent PVC membrane over the paper one, making a double membrane without affecting its transparency. More compromises followed: paper corridors that were an essential ingredient of the scheme were abandoned, and, for some unexplained reason, the exhibition designer inserted a white fabric ceiling that cut the volume interior in half and hid the exposed cardboard-tube grid shell.

But despite all these enforced design compromises, the grid shell survived as a solid demonstration of sustainable design and recycled materials, which, when all was said and done, was the aim of the Expo.

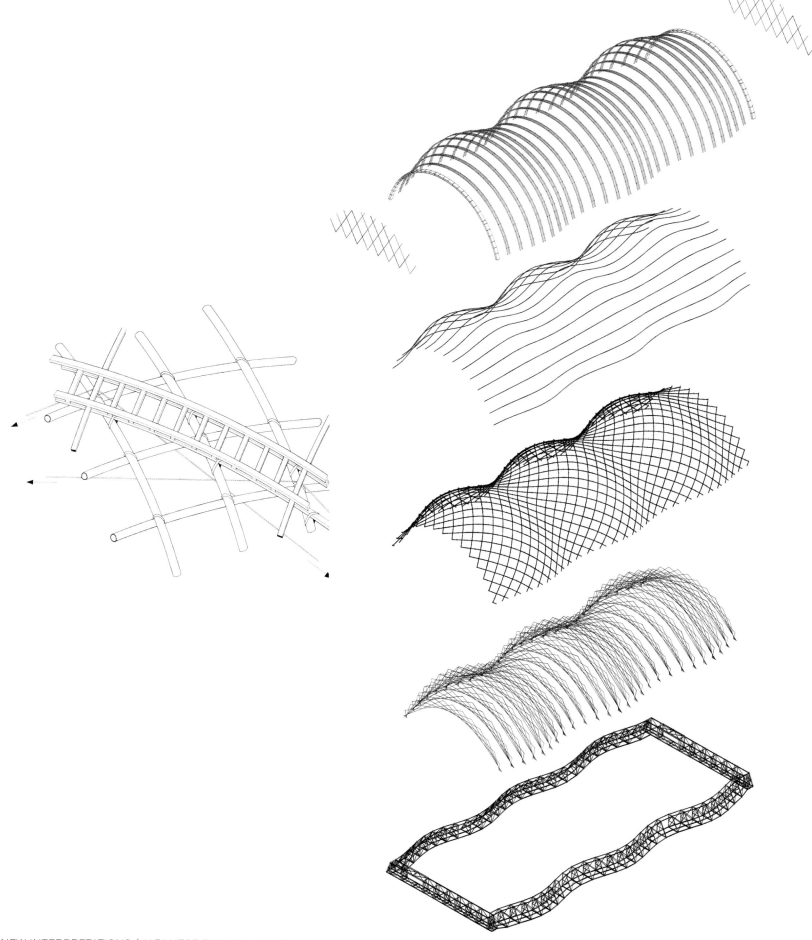

ARCHITECT
Grimshaw Architects, London (UK)

LOCATION
Bodelva, Cornwall (UK)

STRUCTURAL ENGINEER
Anthony Hunt Associates, London (UK)

SERVICES ENGINEER
Arup, London (UK)

BIOME SUPERSTRUCTURE
Mero-Schmidlin, Camberley, Surrey (UK)

ETFE SUBCONTRACTOR
Vector-Foiltec, London (UK)

CLIENT
Eden Project Limited, Bodelva, Cornwall (UK)

COMPLETION
2001

As one of many places along the Cornish Riviera that is free of frost and allows subtropical plants to be grown outdoors, Bodelva is a fitting location for a project that showcases global biodiversity. Initially rejected by the Millennium Commission, the Eden Project, which builds on an earlier venture by archaeologist and record producer Tim Smit, has been a stunning success. Each year it attracts around two million visitors and injects £450 million into a local economy that has been hit hard by the decline of the fishing and mining industries.

Based on Buckminster Fuller's geodesic domes, Nicholas Grimshaw's frothy soap bubbles look like something out of an H.G. Wells novel, and the desolate quarry location further heightens the dramatic impact. There are eight interlinked geodesic domes in the two biomes (one for the humid tropics, the other for temperate environments), which are accessed from the visitor centre on the highest part of the 15-hectare site through a link building. A third biome dedicated to dry tropics is planned for the future.

Grimshaw's lightweight structural strategy has been realized by incorporating Buckminster-fullerenes as the primary structures of the two biomes. The domes are clad with recyclable ETFE foil pillows, an appropriate choice in an innovative, high-profile project devoted to demonstrating biodiversity. The improved insulation properties of ETFE substantially reduce the energy required to heat the two biomes. Both high-tech and low-tech approaches were followed: the frame weight is a mere 22–24kg/m^2 (which would have pleased Fuller enormously), while at the opposite end of the technology spectrum, rammed earth foundation walls were constructed using material excavated from the site.

In the geodesic domes, a primary layer is joined to a secondary layer to form the space-frame. Externally, the primary layer of each dome is divided into an icosahedral geodesic skin made up of hexagonal plates that vary in diameter from 5m to 11m. Each has six straight compressive, galvanized steel tubes that are lightweight and can be easily transported, making it possible to pre-assemble each hexagon before craning it into position and bolting it to its neighbour. The two layers are connected by diagonal circular hollow sections at the node points, so that the assembled layers act structurally as a shell. The meeting of inner and outer structural members form pinned connections, and the dome is anchored at its base to reinforced strip footings around the perimeter.

Designed with ease of movement in mind, access to the biome complex though the Biome Link is direct. The link building consists of two structures within one: a front-facing facility incorporating a raised walkway into the biomes, and a two-storey service area to the rear. At the apex, the point of first contact, a two-storey visitors' centre, arranged to complement the contours of the quarry, is primarily an education facility with multimedia exhibits.

The Eden Project is a powerful demonstration of the ability of membrane structures to embody concepts of efficient and economical resource use in a sustainable and readily expandable way. Much of its success is due to its unique futuristic image, which, besides being attractive, is also highly plausible and fresh.

Clad in three-layer ETFE pillows and covering an area of 23,000m^2, everything about the Eden Project is unconventional and startling.

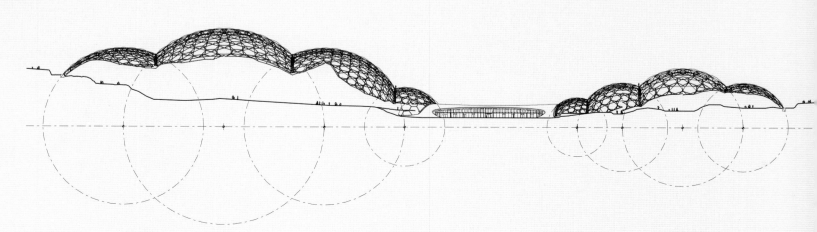

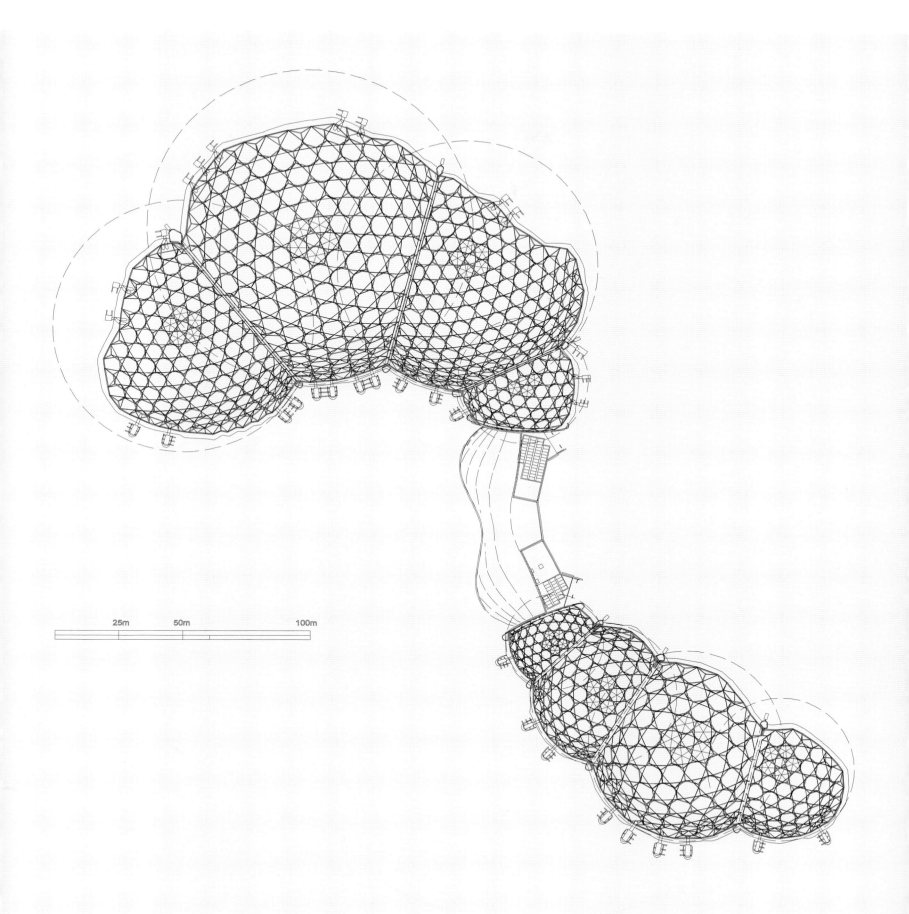

25m   50m   100m

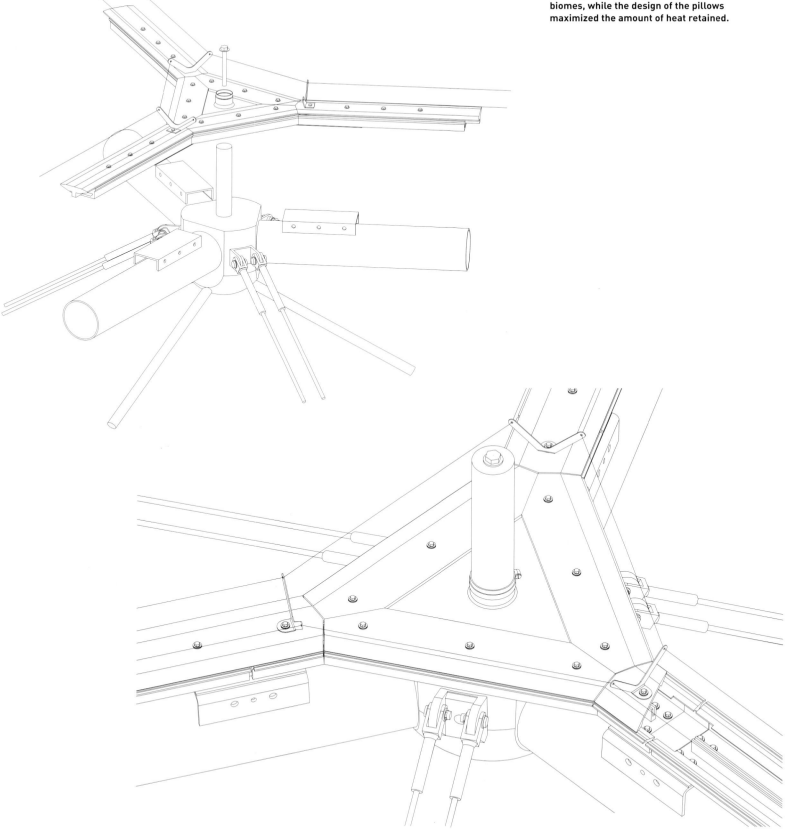

The use of ETFE foil maximized the quantity of light trapped inside the two biomes, while the design of the pillows maximized the amount of heat retained.

The Humid Tropics Biome, at 240m
long, is the largest conservatory in the
world, while the Warm Temperate Biome
exhibits the landscapes of California,
South Africa and the Mediterranean.

THE WATER CUBE

ARCHITECT
PTW Architects, Sydney (Australia)

LOCATION
Beijing (China)

PROJECT MANAGER
Three Gorges Corporation, Yichang,
Hubei (China)

CONSULTANTS
CSCEC + Design, Beijing (China)

ENGINEERING
Arup, Sydney (Australia)

FABRICATOR
Vector-Foiltec, Hampton East,
Victoria (Australia)

CLIENT
Beijing Asset Management,
Beijing (China)

COMPLETION
2006

The design process of Beijing's national swimming stadium, built for the 2008 Olympics and popularly known as the 'Water Cube', explored a range of concepts from curvilinear waves to free-form shapes that evoked images of water in as many ways as possible. The stadium is an anti-monument of supreme simplicity: it is square in plan, signifying 'the order and knowledge of man', with both the swimming pool and seating for 17,000 spectators enclosed in a cubic cage of what appear to be randomly packed soap bubbles. The symbolism is singularly poetic and fitting.

Situated in the Olympic Green opposite the red main stadium by Herzog & de Meuron (p. 130), the blue Water Cube provides a stark contrast. Two-thirds of the building is underground and out of sight; it is only the upper third that is visible and therefore subject to Beijing's extreme climate. The envelope consists of two layers of ETFE foil cushions, one outside and another inside a 3.5m-deep space-frame, with a gap between the two layers for services. In addition, the space-frame had to fulfil seismic design requirements.

The space-frame's geometry corresponds to a century-old teaser posed by Lord Kelvin (1824–1907), the originator of the absolute temperature scale: 'What shape would soap bubbles in a continuous array of soap bubbles be?' It can be imagined as the interstices between soap bubbles, pressed together, that have spontaneously settled into the densest grouping possible. In effect, the Beijing space-frame corresponds to the same minimal configuration suggested by physicists Denis Weaire and Robert Phelan of Trinity College, Dublin. Arup engineers realized that such a

spatial geometry would ensure an economic and repetitive framework. The regular patterns may look fragile, but are in reality extremely robust. They also look uncannily like arrangements of biological cells and mineral crystals, lending a pleasing, organic image. This impression is reinforced by the inner and outer air-filled ETFE bubble cladding.

Four thousand ETFE cells (100,000m^2 in all) were required to wrap the outside and the inside of the space-frame. The foil lets in more light and is a better insulator than glass, cleans itself with every rain shower, and is much more resistant to the weathering effects of sunlight. The Water Cube traps 20 per cent of the solar energy falling on the building; as a result, it is estimated that energy consumption will be reduced by 30 per cent. The cladding also ensures that the interior is well lit during the day, with a consequent savings of up to 55 per cent on energy use. A further refinement is the incorporation of a painted 'frit' on the translucent foil for the differently oriented façades, thus achieving varying degrees of shade depending on solar exposure and thermal requirements.

The Water Cube is a stunning achievement, combining innovative technology with the symbolism of its square form and essential simplicity. At its root is the Chinese idea of harmony: opposites reconciled. Based on an analogy with packed soap bubbles, the minimal spatial form of the highly refined steel space-frame is extremely organic and linked to nature in a quite fundamental way. Together, technology and art make it a remarkable venue, and an especially fitting one for the Olympic swimming and diving events which emphasize the harmony of human movement.

The façade system was modularized to reduce cost by repetition: the number of bubble types was reduced from over 200 to eight standard types for the roof and sixteen for the façades.

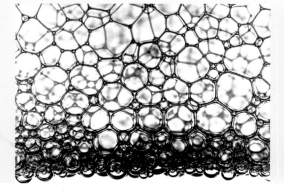

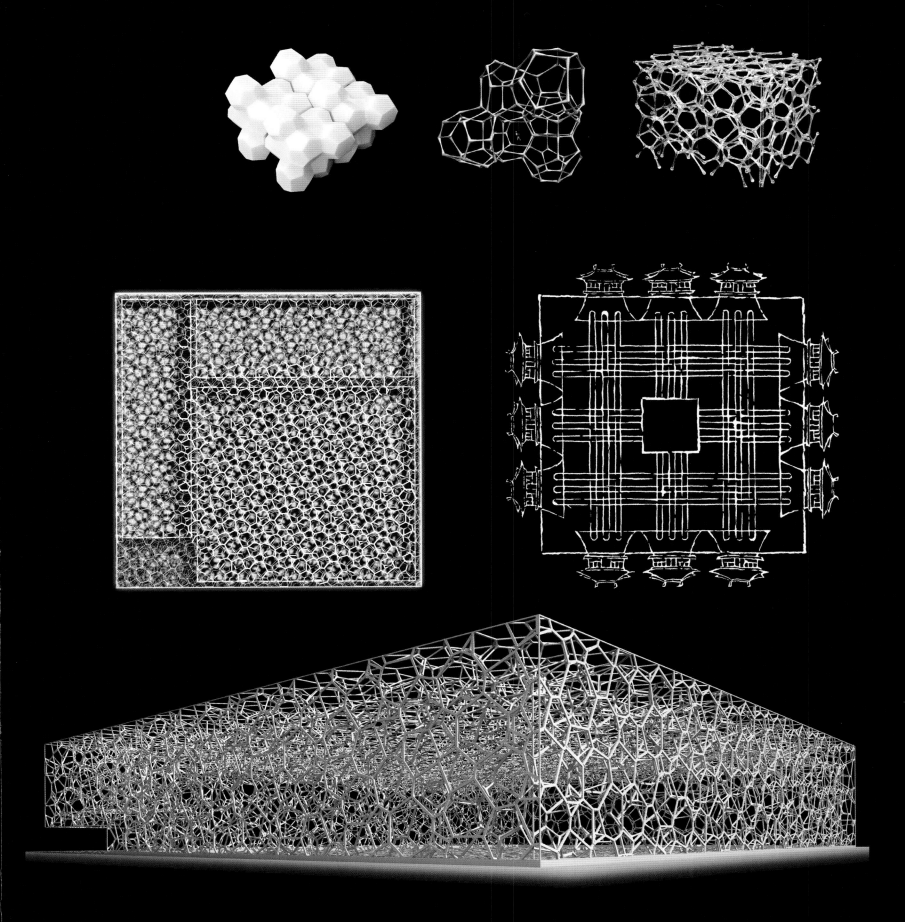

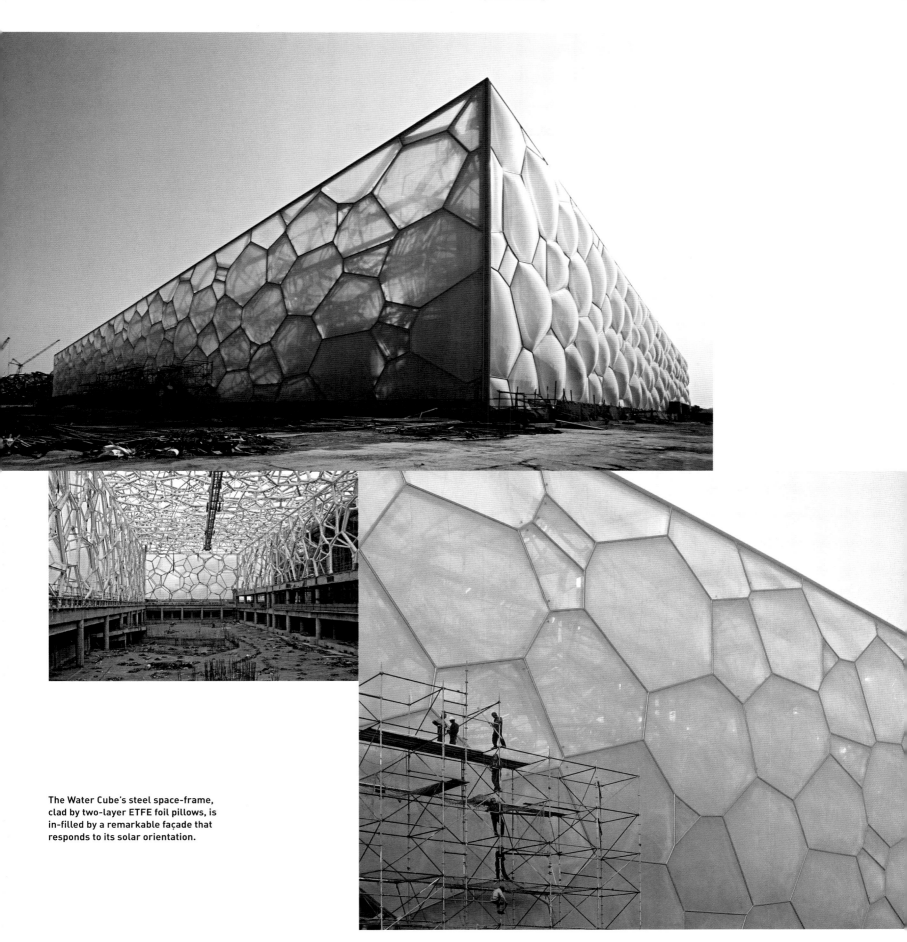

The Water Cube's steel space-frame, clad by two-layer ETFE foil pillows, is in-filled by a remarkable façade that responds to its solar orientation.

ROTATIONAL PNEU

ARTIST
Dominik Baumüller, Munich
(Germany)

LOCATION
Portable

COMPLETION
1997

A new variation of the same umbrella depicted in the bas-reliefs of Ancient Assyria, the Rotational Pneu is a minimal, dynamic shelter reduced to its most fundamental level: a simple, floating canopy without side walls or any enclosure. Artist Dominik Baumüller has removed an essential of the umbrella, the vertical handle. Instead, his shelter consists of two membranes that are inflated by rotating the shape using a small electric motor. The movement pulls air into the cells and inflates them in much the same way that a paraglider wing is stiffened by air flowing over its surface. The faster the flow, the stiffer and more highly inflated the wing becomes.

Structurally, Baumüller's Pneu is an umbrella stabilized by rotational forces which act on the membrane and the enclosed volume of air. To inflate, the structure must be rotated by a motor. The increased cost of rotation is countered by the unique dynamic behaviour of the moving canopy, especially since its shape varies according to the speed of rotation. The draped fabric sculptures of the installation artist Christo were static or moved in quite limited ways, but Baumüller has created a sculpture that is polymorphous.

Since the Rotational Pneu has no rigid structure, it behaves like a soft gyroscope when subjected to wind forces and has a limited maximum speed. It is not, therefore, a real shelter that can be left out in extreme weather.

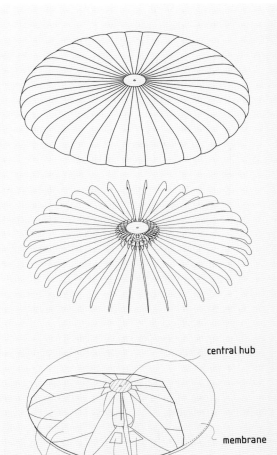

central hub

membrane

vertical ribs

air inlets

The Rotational Pneu's TYVEK polythene fleece (65gm/m²) is powered by an electric motor and can achieve wind speeds of up to 4.5m per second.

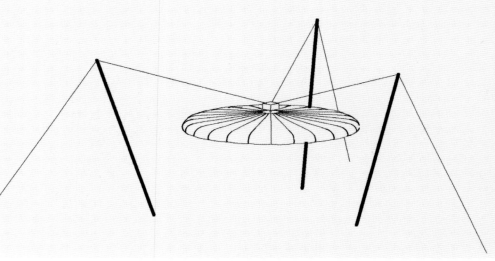

ARTIST
Anish Kapoor, London (UK)

LOCATION
Tate Modern, London (UK)

ENGINEER
Arup, London (UK)

MEMBRANE FABRICATOR
Hightex, Lucerne (Switzerland)

PATTERNING AND COMPENSATION ANALYSIS
Tensys, Bath (UK)

CLIENT
Tate Modern, London (UK)

COMPLETION
2002

Anish Kapoor's *Marsyas* installation was the third in the Unilever Series for Tate Modern's Turbine Hall, a vast space over eight storeys high and 150m long. Kapoor's double-ended trumpet sculpture, on display from October 2002 to April 2003, consisted of three steel rings, joined together by a single span of PVC-coated membrane that made full use of the hall's enormous interior. Shifting from vertical to horizontal and back to vertical, the geometry of the rings determined the overall form. This giant sculpture, a metaphorical 'skin' that takes its name from the satyr of Greek mythology flayed alive by Apollo, can be interpreted as an agonized scream in the emptiness of the Turbine Hall.

Kapoor very quickly realized that he faced a daunting challenge in the height of the hall, and that the only way to deal with the vertical dimension was to give it an intermediate shelf that halved its height, thus helping to establish a human scale between the viewer and the work. In determining how to use the entire length of the Turbine Hall (previous installations had been confined to its eastern end), Kapoor collaborated with Arup's newly formed Advanced Geometry Unit, which had previously worked with such architects as Toyoo Ito, Daniel Libeskind and Shigeru Ban (p. 178).

Ideas explored prior to the wax model were developed further using a virtual reality engine, which employed the latest gaming technology and allowed Kapoor to study the sculpture's texture, colour and lighting through 3D glasses. The final shape was achieved using iterative analytic processes, prototyping and virtual reality, as well as scale models. The membrane was stretched between two 30m-diameter steel rings anchored to the end walls of the hall, and a third ring located 2.5m above the central bridge. This third ring's weight and shape controlled the membrane and managed the overall design. Later, the final horizontal position of the ring was adjusted by adding sandbags to a series of removable panels. The shape was defined using form-finding program FABWIN, which treated the membrane surface as a net of nodes connected by triangles. Each triangle pulled on its three corner nodes with a constant force, which in turn moved the node. This procedure, the equivalent of a soap-film model, was carried out for each of the thousands of nodes and resulted in a surface of uniform curvature in all directions.

The membrane was selected for its strength, cost-effectiveness and ability to be coloured to Kapoor's exacting requirements. The material's behaviour also had to be predicted as accurately as possible, which led to the selection of a 1.8m-wide PVC Type II fabric that was woven and coated under tension to ensure consistent and predictable properties. To realize a continuous, monolithic sculpture, the membrane was fabricated in three sections and then joined with the seams spreading out to the circumference of each ring in radial petals. Tensys, the company that produced the cutting-patterns, shrank the panels according to prestress and squashed them flat so they could be cut. The membrane fabricator, Hightex, then cut the panels and welded them using a high-frequency technique. This was tailoring on a giant scale.

Marsyas illustrated the challenges and advantages of membrane structures, which are very different from conventional construction in terms of speed, economy of material, and innate sculptural possibilities.

The work's PVC-coated membrane, manufactured and coloured in France, had an area of 3,500m² and a span of 140m. The installation took four weeks.

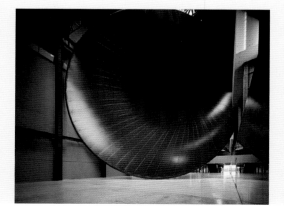

Books

M.M. Ali, *Art of the Skyscraper: The Genius of Fazlur Khan* (New York, 2001).

P.A. Andrews, *Felt Tents and Pavilions: The Nomadic Tradition and its Interaction with Princely Tentage*, 2 vols. (London, 1999).

R. Calzi and P. Corno, *Gypsy Architecture* (Fellbach, 2007).

G. de Bure, *Dominique Perrault* (Basel, 1999).

Directory of Architectural Fabric Structures: Materials, Construction and Location (Glenview, IL, 1984).

Frei Otto, Complete Works: Lightweight Construction, Natural Design, ed. W. Nerdinger (Basel, 2005).

O. Herwig, *Featherweights: Light, Mobile and Floating Architecture* (Munich, 2003).

R. Horn, *Stahl und Lichte: Das Dach des Sony Centre am Potsdamer Platz* (Berlin, 2000).

P. Hyatt, *Local Heroes: Architects of Australia's Sunshine Coast* (Sydney, 2000).

M. Jackson, *Eden: The First Book* (St Ives, 2000).

Y.S. Khan, *Engineering Architecture: The Vision of Fazlur R. Khan* (New York, 2004).

K.-M. Koch and K.J. Habermann, *Membrane Structures: The Fifth Building Material* (Munich, 2004).

R.H. Kronenburg, *FTL: Softness, Movement and Light* (London, 1997).

——, *Houses in Motion: The Genius, History and Development of the Portable Building* (London, 2002).

Membrane Designs and Structures in the World, ed. K. Ishii (Tokyo, 1999).

D. Meyerhöfer, *Mobile Bühneu* (Ludwigsburg, 2000).

P. Møllerup, *Collapsible: The Genius of Space-Saving Design* (Collingdale, PA, 2001).

F. Otto and B. Rash, *Gestalt Finden: Auf dem Weg zu einer Baukunst des Minimalen* (Fellbach, 1995).

K. Powell and R. Rogers, *Richard Rogers: Complete Works*, 3 vols. (London, 1999–2006).

C. Roland, *Frei Otto Structures* (London, 1972).

J. Schlaich and R. Bergermann, *Leicht Weit/Light Structures* (Munich, 2004).

H.-J. Schock, *Segel Folien und Membranen: Innovative Konstruktionen in der Textilen Architektur* (Basel, 2004).

K. Schulte, *Temporary Buildings: The Trade Fair Stand as a Conceptual Challenge* (Corte Madera, CA, 2000).

E. Schunck, et al., *Roof Construction Manual: Pitched Roofs* (Basel, 2003).

J. Sommers, *Gateway to the West: Designing the Passenger Terminal Complex at Denver International Airport* (Mulgrave, Victoria, 2000).

J. Steele, *Ecological Architecture: A Critical History* (London, 2005).

D. Storey, *The Contractor* (London, 1970).

M. Vandenberg, *Soft Canopies* (London, 1996).

B. Walker, *Gabriel Poole: Space in Which the Soul Can Play* (Noosa, Queensland, 1998).

K. Wilson, *A History of Textiles* (Boulder, CO, 1979).

Journals

M. Aoki, 'Habitat nomade d'Anatolie: une architecture autoporteuse', in *L'Architecture d'aujourd'hui* 328 (June 2000): 68–71.

B.N. Bridgens, et al., 'Tensile Fabric Structures: Concepts, Practice and Developments', in *Structural Engineer* 82:14 (2004): 21–27.

B. Burkhardt, 'History of Tent Construction', in 'Membrane Construction', special issue, *Detail* 40:6 (September 2000): 960–64.

T. Carfrae, 'Lightweight Structures', in *Architecture Bulletin* (April/May 2002): 18–19.

R. Clarke, et al., 'Forum Roof, Sony Centre, Berlin: Innovation Beyond "Form Follows Force"', in *Arup Journal* 35:2 (2000): 18–23.

R. Davidson, 'No Fixed Address: Nomads and the Fate of the Planet', special issue, *Quarterly Essay* 24 (December 2006).

Fabric Architecture. Published bimonthly by the Industrial Fabric Association International, Roseville, MN.

B. Forster, 'The Engineered Use of Coated Fabrics in Long-Span Roofs', in *Arup Journal* 20:3 (Autumn 1985): 7–12.

A. Furche, 'Hybrid Roof Structures', in *Detail* 44:7/8 (July/August 2004): 776–82.

E. Happold, et al., 'The Design and Construction of the Diplomatic Club, Riyadh', in *Structural Engineer* 65A/1 (1978): 377–82.

'Lakeside house at Siesta Key', in *Interiors* 110:6 (January 1951): 94–101.

J. Lindner, 'Das Forumdach des Sony Centres am Potsdamer Platz in Berlin', in *Der Stahlbau* 68:12 (December 1999): 975–94.

K. Moritz, 'Membrane Materials in Building', in 'Membrane Construction', special issue, *Detail* 40:6 (September 2000): 1050–58.

'Refurbishment', special issue, *Detail* 41:4 (June 2001).

P. Rice, 'Lightweight Structures: Introduction', in *Arup Journal* 15:3 (October 1980): 2–5.

'Roof Structures', special issue, *Detail* 38:6 (September 1998).

'Roof Structures', special issue, *Detail* 41:5 (July/August 2001).

'Roof Structures', special issue, *Detail* 44:7/8 (July/August 2004).

G. Schmid, 'Properties and Advantages of Membrane Construction in the Context of Refurbishment and Alterations', in *Detail* 43:10 (October 2003): 1159–64.

A.C. Webster, 'Utility, Technology and Expression,' in *The Architectural Review* 191:1149 (November 1992): 68–74.

TensiNews 1–6 (2001–4). Published by TensiNet, Vrije Universiteit Brussel, Faculty of Applied Sciences, Department of Architecture, Brussels.

Other resources

Arbeitskreises Textile Architektur www.textile-architecture.com

Bautex 2000. CD-ROM (Frankfurt am Main, 2000).

Industrial Fabrics Association International www.ifai.com

TensiNet www.tensinet.com

Case-study websites

Allianz Arena [130] www.allianz-arena.de

Burj Al Arab Hotel [170] www.burj-al-arab.com

La Cartuja Olympic Stadium [126] www.eosevilla.com

David L. Lawrence Convention Centre [58] www.pittsburghcc.com

Dynamic Earth Centre [118] www.dynamicearth.co.uk

The Eden Project [184] www.edenproject.com

Hamina Central Bastion [98] www.haminabastioni.fi

Landschaftspark Duisburg-Nord [144] www.landschaftspark.de

Longitude 131° [64] www.longitude131.com.au

Millennium Dome [112] www.millennium-dome.com

Sony Centre [162] www.sonycenter.de

Waldstadion [134] www.commerzbank-arena.de

The Water Cube [190] http://en.beijing2008.cn

Wildscreen-at-Bristol [166] www.wildscreen.org.uk

The following terms are those most often met in membrane structures. The selection is not intended to be complete or exhaustive.

Anisotropic membranes
At present the preferred materials for membrane or tent construction. Their strength, elongation and modulus of elasticity properties vary according to direction.

Anticlastic surface
A surface on which the Gaussian curvature everywhere is negative. See **Gaussian curvature**.

Base fabric
Uncoated base or substrate material of a fabric that determines the strength of the membrane.

Bias
Where a fabric is cut at an angle under 45° to the warp (lengthwise) direction.

Biaxial
Having two axes. A membrane fabric that is stressed in the two principal orthogonal directions.

Buckling resistance
Particular demands are placed on membrane structures that are repeatedly erected and struck, or extended and retracted, as in convertible roofs. Membranes made of fibreglass are unsuitable for such uses. High resistance to buckling is an important determinant of the lifespan of a membrane.

Butt seam
A join between the edges of two fabric pieces, formed by covering the meeting by one or two cover strips.

Cable cuff
Formed by folding over the edge of the material or by attaching a ready-made pocket to the edge of a membrane to take an edge cable.

Cable fitting
Usually fork or eyelet fittings, which are attached to the ends of ropes to connect them to other construction elements.

Catenoids
Minimal surfaces between two rings.

Coating
Any material which is applied to a fabric substrate to improve an important property, such as waterproof capabilities, to make welding more effective and increase fire resistance, thermal or visual properties and durability. A coating is mainly used to protect the base fabric fibres.

Coating adhesion
The adhesion between the fabric and coating. The type of a coating and its thickness will affect fabric strength and such mechanical characteristics as resistance to tearing and durability.

Compensation
In cutting, the shortening of a membrane between its prestressed and unstressed condition must be compensated for differently in the warp and weft directions. While much of the extension of a membrane will be caused by prestressing, creep – induced when the material is first stretched – will, in some instances, also need to be compensated. See **Creep**.

Creep
The increase in elastic–plastic elongation of a material over time, caused by constant tension.

Crimp
The unequal interlacing of the weft over and under the warp threads in a fabric during the weaving process. A textile loaded in the weft direction extends more because the weft thread has more crimp than the warp thread.

Cutting-patterns.
See **Patterning.**

Daylighting
Light produced naturally by sunlight through the membrane.

Decompensation
Additions made to the length of a panel of membrane shortened by compensation, which are made to adjust to particular geometric conditions or to balance concentrations of tensile stresses.

Deformability
Loose textured and light fabrics undergo angular distortion, i.e. the square meshes undergo angular distortion and become diamond-shaped. In contrast to isotropic membranes, their shear stiffness is extremely low, so they behave similarly to cable networks with square meshes under load. Such membranes can be more readily shaped in three dimensions.

Developable
A surface is developable if it can be unfolded onto the flat without the occurrence of stretching or tearing. Only surfaces which are curved in a single direction (null Gaussian curvature), such as a cone or cylinder, are developable.

Elongation
The increase in the length of a material caused by loading. In woven textiles, elongation results from the stretching of the fibres in fixed folds.

Equilibrium shape
The shape assumed by a stretched membrane under specific boundary, support and restraint conditions.

Fabric clamp
A metal profile fixed at the end of a length of fabric, or a clamp plate joint, used to join pieces of fabric.

Fibre
The basic, hair-like material used to make fabrics.

Flutter
Instability caused by the interaction between the wind-load and the load-bearing structure. It happens where there is low prestressing or insufficient curvature.

Flying masts
Struts supported at their bottom by the lower cable of a cable-truss. The extension of a flying-mast may be used to prestress the membrane.

Form-finding
Any process used to discover the optimum equilibrium shape for a construction that satisfies a range of structural parameters, including optimal function, minimal surface or formal factors.

Gaussian curvature
Named after Carl Friedrich Gauss (1777–1855), the product of the

principal curvature from a defined point in a surface. It is negative when a surface is curved in two opposite directions (an anticlastic saddle surface), positive when a surface is completely curved in the same direction, as in a sphere (synclastic surface), null when a surface is curved in only one direction, and is flat in one direction as in a cylinder or cone.

High point
An upwardly projecting point in a spatially curved surface. It may be suspended from above on cables or supported from underneath by masts.

Isotropic membranes
The strength, elongation and modulus of elasticity properties of isotropic membranes are the same in all directions. They usually have one slightly different 'preferred' direction determined by manufacture. Examples are plastic sheets, lattice sheets, metal membranes, rubber membranes, resin-bonded fibres and wood membranes.

Lap seam
A seam made by welding the overlapped edges of two lengths of membrane.

Laying
Unlike a woven fabric where warp and weft threads are interlaced, the threads in one direction are laid on top of the opposite threads underneath.

Light reflectivity
Measurement of the amount of light that is reflected by a surface.

Light transmission
Measurement of the amount of light that passes through a membrane material.

Liner
A secondary membrane suspended below the main membrane or cable-net for thermal or acoustic reasons. Examples are Frei Otto's West Germany Pavilion at Expo 67, and the arenas for the 1972 Olympic Games in Munich.

Low point
A downward projecting point in a spatially curved surface, held down by guys to anchor points in the ground.

Membrane
Pure membranes are only used for very light small- and medium-span structures up to about 50m. The term 'membrane' originally meant a tautly stretched skin. Rubber and sheet-metal membranes, plastic sheets and fleeces have almost equal properties in all directions, and exhibit nearly the same behaviour in all directions while subject to load.

Minimal surface
The smallest surface between closed linear configurations of any shape. The sum of all (positive and negative) radii at each point of the surface is zero. A soap-film will always naturally adopt the shape of a minimal surface. Peak stresses are automatically evened out by the flow of the liquid.

Modulus of elasticity
In most building materials, the relationship of 'stress' (load) to 'strain' (extension) for a body in an elastic state up to the limit of proportionality is constant (linear). In contrast, fabric structures undergo large deflections resulting in non-linear relationships between loads and displacements. The modulus of elasticity is not constant, and instead depends on the tension and the tensile relationship in the warp and weft directions and the loading history.

Node points
Intersection points of structural elements which allow the edges and surfaces of the structure to be geometrically mapped in space.

Non-developable
The property of a curved surface that cannot be unfolded onto a flat plane without stretching or tearing. See **Developable**.

Patterning
The precise geometrical description of a surface or parts onto a flat plane which becomes the basis for the production of spatially curved surfaces. The pattern must be compensated to allow for the increase in sizes of the prestressed dimensions.

Poisson's ratio
Named after Siméon Denis Poisson (1781–1840), a value for the ratio between the long and transverse directions of a membrane. Unlike many other traditional building materials, Poisson's ratio for fabrics depends on the tensile relationship in the warp and weft directions and the loading history.

Prestress
A structural system is considered to be 'prestressed' if stresses exist in the unloaded condition, that is, in the absence of loading due to self-weight or external forces. Prestress is induced by forces which act in the direction of the axis of the system or element, or at right angles to it.

Reinforcement
The strengthening of areas of high local concentrated tension by additional pieces of fabric. Seams also act as simple reinforcement.

Ridge
An elevated line of fold in a curved surface. It often occurs as a ridge-type or in combination with valleys in ridge-and-valley surfaces. See **Valley**.

Ridge-and-valley principle
An alternating parallel or radial layout of opposite curvatures next to each other, created on membrane surfaces that often have only a slight double curvature. The upper curve, which might be compared with the load-bearing cable of a suspension bridge, is called the 'ridge' cable, while the lower 'valley' cable is needed to withstand upward wind-suction forces.

Roped edge
A folded membrane edge detail for inserting a rope, cable or band.

Saddle surface
The basic shape of surface structures loaded in tension. Saddle surfaces are also known as anticlastic surfaces because each set of orthogonal cables or threads are contrarily curved. A continuous saddle surface is anticlastic, or curved in the opposite direction at every point. Since the self-weight is low in comparison with the

magnitude of the prestress, the stresses and shape is elastically secured in space, and therefore the shape is largely independent of orientation. Saddle-shaped surface structures are well known as hyperbolic paraboloids in shell-roof construction. There are many varieties of saddle surfaces depending on the support conditions and edge arrangements: simple saddle surfaces, undulating surfaces, saddle surfaces between arches, hump surfaces.

Scalloped edge
When a flexible edge cable is attached to the boundary of a membrane construction between fixed points, the resulting edge shape is concave or scalloped. The precise curve is determined by the balance of tension forces in the cable and in the surface pulling against it.

Scissor-mast
A pair of masts hinged at the top which is used to lift the tent cloth by drawing the mast feet together to achieve the desired membrane prestress. The Central Algerian black tent has a scissor-mast.

Sectionalizing
Structural membranes are prefabricated in specialized off-site factories. Sectionalizing describes the method of assembling a large membrane from smaller, convenient parts that are held together by clamp plates.

Sewing
Mostly used for uncoated fabrics that are sewn where high strength or a watertight seam is not required in weldable foils or coated fabrics.

Shackle
A U-shaped fitting used to anchor the ends of ropes and straps that allow limited movement in various directions.

Sound absorption
A measurement of the reduction in airborne sound.

Sound reflectivity
The amount of incident sound reflected by a surface.

Spelter
End fitting for cables, formed by passing a cable through a large conical opening and opening it to form a 'brush', whose interstices are coated with liquid zinc (spelter) to create a 'stable'. See **Thimble**.

Surface structures
Structures in which the volume is relatively large in two dimensions, and small in the third dimension. The cross-section of a surface structure may be very thin or it may consist of several parts so that the effective thickness or cross-section, in the case of a fabric membrane, cannot be determined in a straightforward way. All such spatially curved surfaces perform a three-dimensional structural action. They may consist of linear, two-dimensional components.

Swage
A narrow eyelet at the end of a cable through which another cable is inserted, then looped and pressed together.

Textile
Woven fabric, or textiles, consist of an interlaced orthogonal arrangement of warp and weft yarns. The term is used interchangeably with fabric and cloth.

Thimble
Another end fitting for cables, formed by folding a cable over an eyelet that is used as a connecting piece. See **Spelter**.

Turnbuckle
A threaded element used to adjust the length of ropes and tension rods.

Uniaxial
Lying on one of the principal X, Y, Z directions.

UV-degradation
The strength lost in a membrane caused by the coating becoming brittle due to exposure to UV light.

Valley
A sunken inverted fold line in a curved surface. See **Ridge**.

Warp
Lengthwise yarns in a woven fabric.

Weaving
Interlacing warp and weft threads at right angles to each other.

Weft
Crosswise yarns in woven fabric. Also referred to as picks, fill, filling and woof.

Welding
The most common jointing technique used for structural membranes. There are various technologies, such as high-frequency welding or temperature welding.

Wicking
Liquid penetration caused by capillary attraction. In low-wicking and anti-wicking fabrics, a number of threads are specially treated to inhibit the process.

Wrinkles
The presence of wrinkles in a prestressed surface indicates great differences in tensile stress in the principal directions, or as a result of bunching.

DIRECTORY OF ARCHITECTS

Ackermann & Partner [70]
Malsenstraße 57
80638 Munich, Germany
T +49 89 157 000 0
F +49 89 157 000 50
E arch@ackermann-partner.com
W www.ackermann-partner.com

ASP Schweger Assoziierte
Architekten [150]
Valentinskamp 30
20355 Hamburg, Germany
T +49 40 350 959 0
F +49 40 350 959 95
E info@schweger-architekten.eu
W www.schweger-architekten.eu

Mommsenstraße 73
10629 Berlin, Germany
T +49 30 885 972 0
F +49 30 885 972 22
E info.berlin@
    schweger-architekten.eu

Schleißheimer Straße 267
80809 Munich, Germany
T +49 89-35 89 98 - 11
F +49 89-35 89 98 - 95
E info.muenchen@
    schweger-architekten.eu

Shigeru Ban Architects [178]
5-2-4 Matsubara
Setagaya, Tokyo, Japan
T +81 3 3324 6760
F +81 3 3324 6789
E tokyo@shigerubanarchitects.com
W www.shigerubanarchitects.com

Centre Pompidou
place Georges Pompidou
75004 Paris, France
T +33 1 70 71 20 50
F +33 1 70 71 20 51
E europe@
    shigerubanarchitects.com

Dominik Baumüller [196]
Pappenheimstraße 7 Rckg.
80335 Munich, Germany
T +49 89 555 41
E dominik.baumueller@
    beyond-gravity.com
W www.beyond-gravity.com

Cox Richardson Architects [64]
offices worldwide
Level 2, 204 Clarence Street
Sydney NSW 2000, Australia
T +61 2 9267 9599
F +61 2 9264 5844
E sydney@cox.com.au
W www.cox.com.au

Cruz y Ortiz [126]
Santas Patronas 36
41001 Seville, Spain
T +34 954 50 28 25
F +34 954 50 37 04
E mail@cruzyortiz.es
W www.cruz-ortiz.com

Jan Luykenstraat 10
1071 CM Amsterdam
The Netherlands
T +31 20 572 08 56
F +31 20 572 08 49

Fentress Bradburn Architects [92]
421 Broadway
Denver, CO 80203, USA
T +1 303 722 5000
F +1 303 722 5080
E studio@fentressbradburn.com
W www.fentressbradburn.com

1350 Connecticut Ave, NW
Suite 1250
Washington, DC 20036, USA
T +1 202 337 5100
F +1 202 337 5139

Grimshaw Architects [184]
57 Clerkenwell Road
London EC1M 5NG, UK
T +44 20 7291 4141
F +44 20 7291 4194
E info@grimshaw-architects.com
W www.grimshaw-architects.com

100 Reade Street
New York, NY 10013, USA
T +1 212 791 2501
F +1 212 791 2173

494 LaTrobe Street
Melbourne, Victoria 3000, Australia
T +61 3 9321 2600
F +61 3 9321 2611

Herzog & de Meuron
Architekten [130]
Rheinschanze 6
4056 Basel, Switzerland
T +41 61 385 5757
F +41 61 385 5758
E info@herzogdemeuron.ch

Hopkins Architects
[76, 80, 118, 166]
offices worldwide
27 Broadley Terrace
London NW1 6LG, UK
T +44 20 7724 1751
F +44 20 7723 0932
E mail@hopkins.co.uk
W www.hopkins.co.uk

Ingenhoven Overdiek
Architekten [108]
Plange Mühle 1
40221 Düsseldorf, Germany
T +49 21 130 101 01
E info@ingenhovenarchitekten.de
W www.ingenhoven-overdiek.de

Anish Kapoor [198]
c/o Lisson Gallery
29 & 52–54 Bell Street
London NW1 5BY, UK
T +44 20 7724 2739
F +44 20 7724 7124
E contact@lisson.co.uk
W www.lissongallery.com

Roy Mänttäri [98]
Kapteeninkatu 8 F 12
00140 Helsinki, Finland
T +358 9 625 034
E roy.manttari@ark.inet.fi

John McAslan & Partners [158]
49 Princes Place
London W11 4QA, UK
T +44 20 7727 2663
F +44 20 7221 8835
E mailbox@mcaslan.co.uk
W www.mcaslan.co.uk

St John's House
2–10 Queen Street
Manchester M2 5JB, UK
T +44 161 833 2037
F +44 161 833 2038
E manchester@mcaslan.co.uk

Murphy/Jahn Architects [162]
35 East Wacker Drive, 3rd Floor
Chicago, IL 60601, USA
T +1 312 427 7300
F +1 312 332 0274
E info@murphyjahn.com
W www.murphyjahn.com

Oscar Niemeyer [46]
Fundação Oscar Niemeyer
Rua Conde Lages, 25 - Glória
Rio de Janeiro, Brazil
T/F +55 21 2509 1844
E fundacao@niemeyer.org.br
W www.niemeyer.org.br

Planinghaus Architekten [144]
Heidelberger Straße 84
64285 Darmstadt, Germany
T +49 61 519 631 51
F +49 61 519 631 52
E post@planinghaus.de
W www.planinghaus.de

PTW Architects [190]
offices worldwide
Level 17, 9 Castlereagh Street
Sydney NSW 2000, Australia
T +61 2 9232 5877
F +61 2 9221 4139
E info@ptw.com.au
W www.ptw.com.au

Richard Rogers Partnership [112]
*now known as Rogers Stirk
Harbour + Partners*
Thames Wharf, Rainville Road
London W6 9HA, UK
T +44 20 7385 1235
F +44 20 7385 8409
E enquiries@rsh-p.com
W www.rsh-p.com

Samyn & Partners [86, 102]
1537 Chaussée de Waterloo
1180 Brussels, Belgium
T +32 2 347 90 60
E sai@samynandpartners.be
W www.samynandpartners.be

Álvaro Siza [50]
Rua de Aleixo 53
4150-043 Porto, Portugal
T +351 2 610 8574

Souto Moura Arquitectos [54]
Rua de Aleixo 53
4150-043 Porto, Portugal
T +351 2 618 7547
F +351 2 610 8092
E souto.moura@mail.telepac.pt

Silja Tillner [140]
Margaretenplatz 7/2/1
1050 Vienna, Austria
T +43 1 310 68 59
F +43 1 310 68 59 15
E tw@tw-arch.at
W www.tw-arch.at

Rafael Viñoly Architects [58]
50 Vandam Street
New York, NY 10013, USA
T +1 212 924 5060
F +1 212 924 5858
E info@rvapc.com
W www.rvapc.com

8563 Higuera Street
Culver City, CA 90232, USA
T +1 310 839 9968

2-4 Exmoor Street
London W10 6BD, UK
T +44 20 8206 6200
F +44 20 8206 6201

Von Gerkan, Marg & Partner [134]
Elbchaussee 139
22763 Hamburg, Germany
T +49 40 881 510
F +49 40 881 511 77
E hamburg-e@gmp-architekten.de
W www.gmp-architekten.de

**W.S. Atkins & Partners
Overseas** [170]
offices worldwide
P.O. Box 5620
Dubai, United Arab Emirates
T +971 4 4059 300
F +971 4 4059 301
E office.dubai@atkinsglobal.com
W www.atkinsglobal.com

Plans and drawings supplied by the architects and designers, unless otherwise specified. All other photographs supplied by the author.

© Matteo Piazza 2, 88–91; © The Trustees of The British Museum 12; Souto Moura Arquitectos 44; © Edifice/Corbis (Gillian Darley) 46; Richard Bryant/Arcaid 47 (above left and right); © Richard Bryant/Arcaid/Corbis 47 (below), 48–49; Arquivo Fotográfico Municipal de Lisboa 50–53; AFP/Getty Images (Sven Nackstrand) 54; Getty Images (Laurence Griffiths) 55 (above); AFP/Getty Images (Stringer) 55 (below); © Christian Richters 56–57; © 2004 Brad Feinknopf 58–61; Patrick Bingham Hall 62, 66–69; Cox Richardson Architects 64; Klaus Kinold 72 (above), 73 (above and below left); Simone Rosenberg 72 (below); Detail 73 (below right); Hans Neudecker 74–75; M. Schinzler 75 (right); © Timothy Soar 77–79; Morley van Sternberg 81–83; Keith Hunter 84, 120–123; © J. Bauters 86; Fentress Bradburn Architects 94–97; Roy Mäntärri 100, 101; © Marie-Françoise Plissart 104, 106–107, 107 (right); Samyn & Partners 105; Ingenhoven Overdiek Architekten 110–111; © London Aerial Photo Library/Corbis (Sandy Stockwell) 114, 188–189; © Jason Hawkes/Corbis 115 (above); © Büro Happold/Mandy Reynolds 115 (below left and right); © Pawel Libera/Corbis 116–17; Von Gerkan, Marg & Partner 124, 136–139; Duccio Malagamba 126, 127, 128–129; Getty Images (Mike Hewitt) 129 (right); Vector-Foiltec 130–133, 143, 187, 188 (left); Covertex 141; Monika Nikolic 142; © Planinghaus Architekten 146–149; © Bernhard Kroll/ASP 152, 153; Bongarts/Getty Images (Stuart Franklin) 154–155; © Hopkins Architects 156, 168 (above), 168–169; View (Peter Cook) 159–161; © Robert Lyons 164; Murphy/Jahn Architects 165; View (Dennis Gilbert) 168 (below); Richard Powers 171, 172–173, 174–175; © Attar Maher/Corbis Sygma 172 (left); Ben McMillan 176, 192, 193 (above), 194–195; Büro Happold/Adam Wilson 178, 180, 182–183; View (Roland Halbe/Artu) 181; PTW Architects 193 (below, left and right); Tobias Lehn 197 (top, all, and middle, all); Dominik Baumüller 197 (below); John Riddy, London/© Tate 198, 200–201; Tate Photography/Marcus Leith and Andrew Dunkley 199.